Hands-On Dark Web Analysis

Learn what goes on in the Dark Web, and how to work with it

Sion Retzkin

BIRMINGHAM - MUMBAI

Hands-On Dark Web Analysis

Commissioning Editor: Gebin George
Acquisition Editor: Heramb Bhavsar
Content Development Editor: Ronn Kurien
Technical Editor: Prachi Sawant
Copy Editor: Safis Editing
Project Coordinator: Jagdish Prabhu
Proofreader: Safis Editing
Indexer: Rekha Nair
Graphics: Tom Scaria
Production Coordinator: Jyoti Chauhan

First published: December 2018

Production reference: 1241218

Published by Packt Publishing Ltd.
Livery Place
35 Livery Street
Birmingham
B3 2PB, UK.

ISBN 978-1-78913-336-3

www.packtpub.com

mapt.io

Mapt is an online digital library that gives you full access to over 5,000 books and videos, as well as industry leading tools to help you plan your personal development and advance your career. For more information, please visit our website.

Why subscribe?

- Spend less time learning and more time coding with practical eBooks and Videos from over 4,000 industry professionals

- Improve your learning with Skill Plans built especially for you

- Get a free eBook or video every month

- Mapt is fully searchable

- Copy and paste, print, and bookmark content

Packt.com

Did you know that Packt offers eBook versions of every book published, with PDF and ePub files available? You can upgrade to the eBook version at www.packt.com and as a print book customer, you are entitled to a discount on the eBook copy. Get in touch with us at customercare@packtpub.com for more details.

At www.packt.com, you can also read a collection of free technical articles, sign up for a range of free newsletters, and receive exclusive discounts and offers on Packt books and eBooks.

Contributors

About the author

Sion Retzkin is an IT and security professional with over 20 years' experience in various technical and business roles. Sion was born in New York City, and has lived, studied, and worked internationally. Sion also delivers training to other professionals on the topics he's mastered, sharing his passion for security, ethical hacking, and information systems. With multiple certifications under his belt, Sion feels comfortable both in the boardroom, meeting customers, and working hands-on.

Today, he works at Pcysys, as director of customer success, which allows him to continue to do what he loves.

I would like to thank Meytal, my wife and love of my life, for putting up with long nights of writing and thinking (sometimes out loud), on how I can make this book effective and interesting. To my sons, who loaned their father to this book, and for whom I wrote it, I love you. Also, thanks to my reviewer, Rishalin Pillay, for helping me in writing chapters, and to my editors in Packt, who offered ideas, improvements and encouragement, during my writing.

About the reviewer

Rishalin Pillay, with in excess of 11 years of cybersecurity experience, has acquired a vast number of skills consulting for Fortune 500 companies while participating in projects performing tasks in network security design, implementation, and vulnerability analysis. He holds many certifications that demonstrate his knowledge and expertise in the cybersecurity field, such as CISSP, CCNP Security, CCSPA, MCSE, MCT, A+ and Network+

Rishalin currently works at a large-scale software company as a senior cybersecurity engineer.

Packt is searching for authors like you

If you're interested in becoming an author for Packt, please visit `authors.packtpub.com` and apply today. We have worked with thousands of developers and tech professionals, just like you, to help them share their insight with the global tech community. You can make a general application, apply for a specific hot topic that we are recruiting an author for, or submit your own idea.

Table of Contents

Preface

The World Wide Web is divided into three areas: the Surface Web, the Deep Web, and the Dark Web. The Deep Web and Dark Web are the two areas that are not accessible through general search engines or browsers. This provides several advantages, such as anonymity and privacy, but it also provides people performing illicit, illegal, or nefarious activities with the same benefits. IT and security professionals also gain benefits by accessing these areas.

This book will initially introduce you to the concept of the Deep Web and the Dark Web and will examine their significance. Then, we will deep dive into the recommended ways to access them, by using various operating systems and tools such as the Tor browser. We will also discuss what data can be obtained there, best practices for using the tools for the best effect, and who uses the Deep Web and the Dark Web.

By the end of this book, you will have hands-on experience of working with the Deep Web and the Dark Web.

Who this book is for

This book is aimed at IT and security professionals, security analysts, and any stakeholder interested in learning the concepts of the Deep Web and the Dark Web. Some technical acumen is necessary for the hands-on parts of this book, such as internet browsing, the concept and use of virtual machines, and installing operating systems. The book includes step-by-step instructions, with screenshots of all the hands-on chapters.

What this book covers

Chapter 1, *Understanding the Deep and Dark Web*, starts by looking at where it all started, and we will talk about the terminology—what is the Deep Web? What is the Dark Web? We will also talk about the difference between the Deep Web and the Dark Web, and examine the reason behind the names and what can be done there.

Chapter 2, *Working with the Deep Web*, discusses using the Deep Web and the Dark Web. For example, how to access the Deep Web and the Dark Web, and what really goes on there? How can there be so many sites out there? In this chapter, we'll discuss how the Deep Web and Dark Web are used.

Chapter 3, *The Future of the Dark Web*, covers the usage trends in the Dark Web. We will also talk about how it is used today and where will it go from here. We will learn about what to expect in the future from the Deep Web and the Dark Web. We will learn about the future benefits (or dangers) we can gain from the uncharted territory of the Dark Web.

Chapter 4, *Installing a Linux Virtual Machine (VM)*, explains how to install a Linux virtual machine.

Chapter 5, *Accessing the Dark Web with the Tor Browser*, will help you to learn about, install, and configure the Tor browser on a Linux distribution.

Chapter 6, *Installing Tails OS*, outlines another operating system that is useful for accessing the Deep Web—Tails OS. It is a live operating system that you can start on almost any computer from a USB stick or a DVD. In this chapter, we'll focus on installing Tails OS and accessing the Dark Web with it.

Chapter 7, *Installing Whonix*, covers another operating system that's worth mentioning: Whonix. Whonix is designed for advanced security and privacy. It's a heavily reconfigured Linux Debian that runs inside multiple virtual machines, providing a substantial layer of protection from malware and IP address leaks. Whonix is the only operating system designed to be run inside a VM and paired with Tor. In this chapter, we'll learn how to install and use Whonix to browse the Dark Web.

Chapter 8, *Installing Qubes OS*, covers a Xen-based operating system that is also considered extremely secure: Qubes OS, which will be the focus of this chapter. Qubes OS operates under the assumption that it has already been breached, so every application is run in its own virtual environment. In this chapter, we will learn how to install and use Qubes OS to access the Deep Web.

Chapter 9, *What Goes on in the Dark Web – Case Studies*, provides several examples of how the Dark Web is used in order to outline the dangers (and benefits) of going there. Anyone can access the Dark Web and, in this chapter, we will break down the types of people who access it, and why.

Chapter 10, *The Dangers of the Dark Web*, discusses the things that are lurking in the Dark Web. What are the dangers? How do we avoid them? These are probably the type of questions you've asked yourself when contemplating the Dark Web. Many people view the Dark Web as an evil place, teeming with malicious hooded hackers, just waiting for us to enter. In this chapter, we'll learn what the risks are in the Dark Web, and how to avoid them.

Chapter 11, *Using the Dark Web for Your Business*, moves on from who uses the Deep Web and Dark Web, and why. Now, let's learn how we can use them ourselves, to help us perform tasks, to help in our career, and more.

To get the most out of this book

You should have a USB stick and a computer you are willing to format, or a computer with enough resources to create virtual machines.

Download the color images

We also provide a PDF file that has color images of the screenshots/diagrams used in this book. You can download it here: `https://www.packtpub.com/sites/default/files/downloads/9781789133363_Color Images.pdf`.

Conventions used

There are a number of text conventions used throughout this book.

`CodeInText`: Indicates code words in text, database table names, folder names, filenames, file extensions, pathnames, dummy URLs, user input, and Twitter handles. Here is an example: "Double-click on the `Start-tor-browser.desktop` file to launch Tor Browser"

A block of code is set as follows:

```
html, body, #map {
 height: 100%;
 margin: 0;
 padding: 0
 }
```

Any command-line input or output is written as follows:

```
sudo apt install gnupg
```

Bold: Indicates a new term, an important word, or words that you see onscreen. For example, words in menus or dialog boxes appear in the text like this. Here is an example: "Now, plug in the second USB stick, go to **Applications** | **Tails** | **Tails Installer** (in Tails OS), and install Tails on it."

Warnings or important notes appear like this.

Tips and tricks appear like this.

Get in touch

Feedback from our readers is always welcome.

General feedback: If you have questions about any aspect of this book, mention the book title in the subject of your message and email us at customercare@packtpub.com.

Errata: Although we have taken every care to ensure the accuracy of our content, mistakes do happen. If you have found a mistake in this book, we would be grateful if you would report this to us. Please visit www.packt.com/submit-errata, selecting your book, clicking on the Errata Submission Form link, and entering the details.

Piracy: If you come across any illegal copies of our works in any form on the Internet, we would be grateful if you would provide us with the location address or website name. Please contact us at copyright@packt.com with a link to the material.

If you are interested in becoming an author: If there is a topic that you have expertise in and you are interested in either writing or contributing to a book, please visit authors.packtpub.com.

Reviews

Please leave a review. Once you have read and used this book, why not leave a review on the site that you purchased it from? Potential readers can then see and use your unbiased opinion to make purchase decisions, we at Packt can understand what you think about our products, and our authors can see your feedback on their book. Thank you!

For more information about Packt, please visit packt.com.

Disclaimer

The information within this book is intended to be used only in an ethical manner. Do not use any information from the book if you do not have written permission from the owner of the equipment. If you perform illegal actions, you are likely to be arrested and prosecuted to the full extent of the law. Packt Publishing does not take any responsibility if you misuse any of the information contained within the book. The information herein must only be used while testing environments with proper written authorizations from appropriate persons responsible.

Understanding the Deep and Dark Web 1

The Deep Web, the Dark Web, the Dark Net.

We've all heard about them, if it's from a movie, TV show, the news, or even a friend or a neighbor. Most people view them as the same thing, which is as a depraved and illegal area on the internet, where sex-traffickers, drug dealers, weapons dealers, and others lurk in wait for innocent users.

The truth is very far from this. In this book, we'll understand what the Deep Web, the Dark Web, and the Dark Net are, how to access them safely and securely, who uses them and, ultimately, how we can use them for beneficial and good uses, rather than what the media publishes about them.

But, in order to fully understand them, we need to understand the origins of the internet, and how it works, as they are intrinsically connected.

We will cover the following topics in this chapter:

- The origin of the internet
- The Deep Web
- The Dark Web

The origin of the internet

Many of you might have heard that the internet was originally created by DARPA, The Defense Advanced Research Projects Agency, which is part of the United States Department of Defense, and is responsible for development of new technologies for use by the US military.

But, this is not necessarily the first appearance of the internet. Back then, it was more of an **intra**-net, as all the computers were on the same network. It all depends on how you define the internet. Nowadays, the internet is defined as a *network of networks* or multiple interconnected computer networks that provide communication and information capabilities, using standardized communication protocols such as **Transport Control Protocol/Internet Protocol (TCP/IP**)

Some say that the internet began after packet switching technology was created, others say it was after TCP/IP was launched, and yet others claim that the origins of the internet were in the UK, not in the US.

The starting date of the internet (or rather ARPANET, as it was known then) is also inconclusive. Although most people agree that it was launched in 1969, there is concrete evidence that it originated even earlier.

The following diagram is a model of ARPANET from 1982:

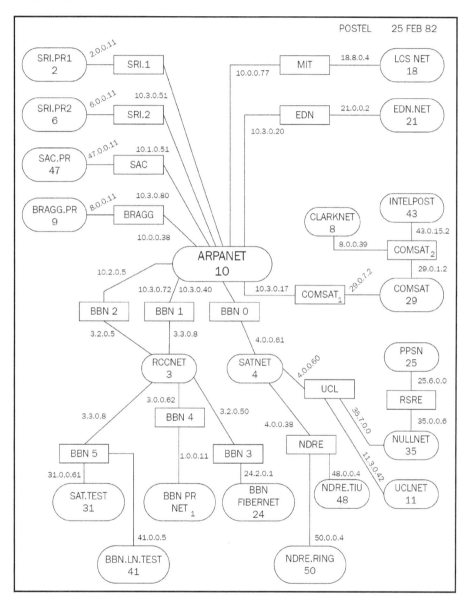

In August 1962, J.C.R. Licklider of MIT began discussing his *Galactic Network* concept. His idea was to create a globally interconnected set of computers through which anyone could quickly access data and programs from anywhere in the world.

This was based on packet switching technology, a way by which messages can travel from point to point across a network. He even got to the point where he implemented a packet switch connecting a set of host computers. This technology was already a concept in 1965, proposed by an Englishman called Donald Davies, but it never got funded. ARPANET adopted his ideas and continued from there.

Additionally, a Frenchman called Louis Pouzin introduced the idea of datagrams (data + telegram—a basic transfer unit in a packet-switched network) around that time.

In 1968, The National Physical Laboratory in the UK set up the first test network for packet switching. This inspired DARPA to work on ARPANET.

Whatever the origin of the internet, the original intent of ARPANET was to allow people in remote locations to use the processing power of remote computers for scientific calculations.

In December 1970, the initial ARPANET host-to-host protocol, called the **Network Control Protocol** (**NCP**), was added to the network, and in 1972, email technology was introduced.

Additionally, in 1972, the concept of open-architecture networking was introduced, providing the basis for networks of different technologies to be able to connect (this also sowed the seeds for the OSI model in the future).

In 1978, TCP/IPv4 was released, and was added to ARPANET in 1983. This was the first actual internet, the basis of the internet which we know and love today.

So, what is the internet?

As shown in the above diagram, it's a vast, global network of interconnected networks that uses TCP/IP to communicate.

There are literally millions upon millions of networks connected, and nowadays the networks are no longer only computer-based. **internet of Things** (**IoT**) technology connects devices that aren't computers to the internet, as well.

You may also be familiar with the term **World Wide Web**.

Also called simply *the web*, it's a way of accessing information, such as web resources and documents, by accessing **Uniform Resource Locators** (**URLs**) and Hypertext links, using various protocols (such as **Hypertext Transfer Protocol** (**HTTP**)) to allow applications (such as a browser) to access and share information.

A protocol is a set of rules that dictates how to format, transmit, and receive data so network devices can communicate, regardless of their infrastructure, design, or standards.

Browsers were created in 1990 by English scientist Tim Berners-Lee during his employment at CERN, in Switzerland.

The internet is the infrastructure upon which the World Wide Web can be used.

Now, after we've understood what the internet is and how it began, let's talk about the Deep Web.

As you know, Google and other search engines (Bing, Yahoo, and so on) index sites by *crawling* them and incorporating the data crawled into their index servers. The search engines then organize the data by context, according to their logic, and enter the data into a base of algorithms that make up the search engine.

This data, indexed by a search engine, and accessed via the World Wide Web (also called the Surface Web), is actually only a small part of the entire internet.

Many people like to view the internet as an island or a glacier at sea, and only part of it is viewable above the surface of the water:

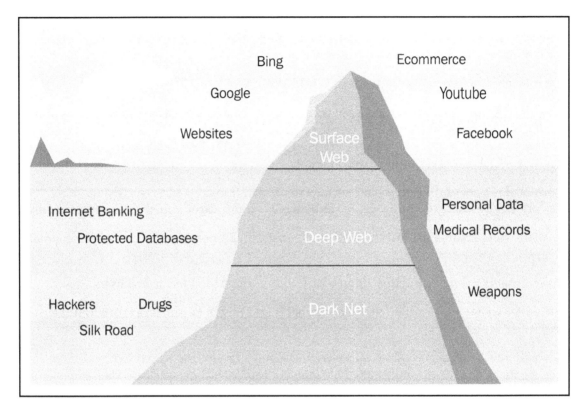

Surface Web, Deep Web, and Dark Net

As you can see in the preceding diagram , the Surface Web is the tip that's visible above the water.

This area can be indexed by search engines, and contains all the publicly available information, documents, and content.

Sadly, many people who aren't tech-savvy or aren't aware, and even companies, allow their data to be indexed, which provides information to attackers, helping them gain access, locate files and data, and more.

For example, an attacker might want to cause reputational damage to a certain business. Performing reconnaissance, the attacker discovers a weakness to be exploited—the business' backups procedure saves the backup of their customer database to their public website for 24 hours before it is moved to a secure location. This allows the backup to be crawled by search engines. The attacker can use a search engine to find the database file on the business' website. Since the website is indexed, the search engine is able to provide the results to the attacker. The attacker can then simply download and use the file(s) for malicious purposes.

The Deep Web

If the Surface Web is the indexable part of the internet, the Deep Web is everything else. The Deep Web is the area on the internet that can't be, or isn't, indexed. And it's much, much bigger. This is because the Deep Web includes much more than what you probably think. Remember—the internet isn't the World Wide Web (Surface Web). It's the infrastructure over which the Surface Web is accessed. So, the Deep Web (most of it, anyway, but we'll talk about that soon), also exists on the internet. Any website or system that requires login credentials is part of the Deep Web.

Organizational information and intranets of businesses, academic institutes, governmental departments, and others, are also part of the Deep Web, as are websites that specifically prevent search engines from indexing parts of the website, such as Google Scholar, or Amazon.

The following screenshot displays searching for `deep web` in Google Scholar:

As you can see, there are results.

After clicking the **Accessing the deep web** link, note the following:

We arrive at a login screen. So, the article itself is on the Deep Web, but its title and metadata was indexed by Google, and therefore was returned as a search result.

Now, let's understand what we just read—the Deep Web is accessible using any standard browser, but is not indexed by search engines, so you usually need to either enter a username and password to access the content or be in a specific network (company or university network, for example).

But what about the Dark Web?

The Dark Web

As the Surface Web, or WWW, is on the internet, the Dark Web exists on the Dark Net (or rather, multiple darknets).

It's important to point out that the terms Dark Web and Dark Net aren't the same thing. Dark Net was a term used in the 1970s', for networks that were isolated from ARPANET, mainly for security purposes, such as compartmentalization. They were configured to be able to receive external data, but they were hidden from the ARPANET network listings and wouldn't respond to networking inquiries, such as ping requests.

Over time, the term was also used for overlay networks, which are essentially networks that utilize software and hardware to create multiple layers of abstraction. These layers are run over multiple separate and discrete network layers on top, or over a common network (hence *overlay*), accessible only with special browsers or software, or where their IP addresses aren't globally routable. A few examples of such overlay networks are Tor, the **Invisible internet Project** (**I2P**), or FreeNet.

So, you can view the Dark Net as the infrastructure underneath the Dark Web, which is the content and websites that you can access only with the specialized software I mentioned, and which we will discuss as we proceed in this chapter, and in the book.

To give you an example of a Dark Net, I'll mention Tor, or The Onion Router. It's essentially a distributed network of servers or hosts, where users, traffic is bounced around between various routers.

This makes it hard to monitor the data, enhancing anonymity, privacy, and security.

 A comparison between TOR and I2P can be found here: `https://geti2p.net/en/comparison/tor`.

The following diagram is from the Argonne National Laboratory website, and it demonstrates what I just mentioned in a graphical manner:

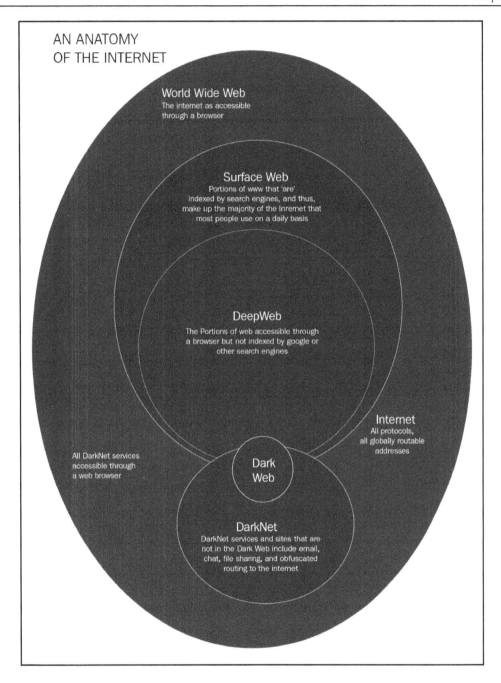

AN ANATOMY
OF THE INTERNET

World Wide Web
The internet as accessible
through a browser

Surface Web
Portions of www that 'are'
indexed by search engines, and thus,
make up the majority of the Inrernet that
most people use on a daily basis

DeepWeb
The Portions of web accessible through
a browser but not indexed by google or
other search engines

Internet
All protocols,
all globally routable
addresses

All DarkNet services
accessible through
a web browser

Dark
Web

DarkNet
DarkNet services and sites that are
not in the Dark Web include email,
chat, file sharing, and obfuscated
routing to the internet

As you can see, the internet encompasses the Deep Web, which is in (or under) the Surface Web, and the Dark Web, which is on the Dark Net (yet another part of that magnificent *network of networks* known as the internet).

We will discuss who uses the Dark Web, and how, in this book, but let's take a high-level look first, before we dive in.

Law enforcement

I'll start with law enforcement, since most people believe that the Dark Web is illegal, either to access, or due to what goes on there. So, I want to reassure you—just as in the real world, so also in the Dark Web do we have law enforcement. Due to its anonymity and privacy, criminals use the Dark Web. And where there are criminals, there are police. Due to the anonymity, criminals can create online marketplaces for drugs, weapons, and other illegal material. Law enforcement agencies such as the FBI and many others utilize the Dark Net for sting operations, to capture criminals. They leverage the Dark Web themselves, reducing the exposure of governmental IP addresses and ensuring their anonymity on the Dark Web, thus increasing their effectiveness.

One of the things that law enforcement agencies do is to take down illegal marketplaces. Many agencies attempt to take over illegal marketplaces, enabling them to not only deter the sale of illegal materials, but to also track the buyers and sellers of such materials.

Journalism

Journalists often need to report a story, only to be at risk for various reasons. Using the Dark Web, journalists are able to report and share information anonymously and securely. Services such as *Secure Drop* exist to enable organizations to receive documents and tips from anonymous sources. There are a number of major news agencies that use Secure Drop.

Secure Drop keeps a directory of active instances, and you can view this here: `https://securedrop.org/directory/`.

Privacy

Privacy is a top concern for many people today. With the rise of interconnected devices and data being moved to the cloud, privacy concerns are on the rise.

When you browse an average website, there are a number of tracking actions that the website can perform. For example, a website can leverage the following:

- Tracking cookies
- Fingerprinting of the browser
- Referral links
- IP addresses
- Tracking scripts

Using the information obtained, websites can perform a few things, such as targeted advertising.

By using the Dark Web, people ensure that they are keeping their legal online activity anonymous. There is no need to worry about websites tracking your location or online activity.

Criminals

Since the Dark Web offers anonymity and security, criminals often use it to protect themselves and to prevent capture. Although law enforcement agencies operate within the Dark Web, it does mean that they stop all criminals from partaking in criminal activities.

Drugs and illegal substances

There are a variety of marketplaces within the dark web that sell a vast array of drugs and illegal substances. One of the most popular marketplaces is *Silk Road*.

Silk Road started back in 2011 and was used to sell magic mushrooms at first. The marketplace started to grow and moved on towards other drugs and commodities. Silk Road has progressed to version 3.1. The previous versions were also taken down either by law enforcement or by the admins.

Another marketplace that is very popular is the *Wallstreet Market*. This marketplace offers a variety of goods, as can be seen here:

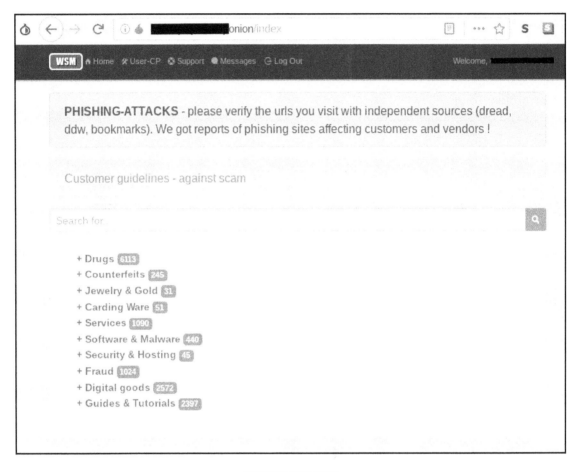

Wallstreet Market Categories

Counterfeit goods

Within the Dark Web, you can find a wealth of counterfeit goods. These range from counterfeit electronics, currency, to even identification documents:

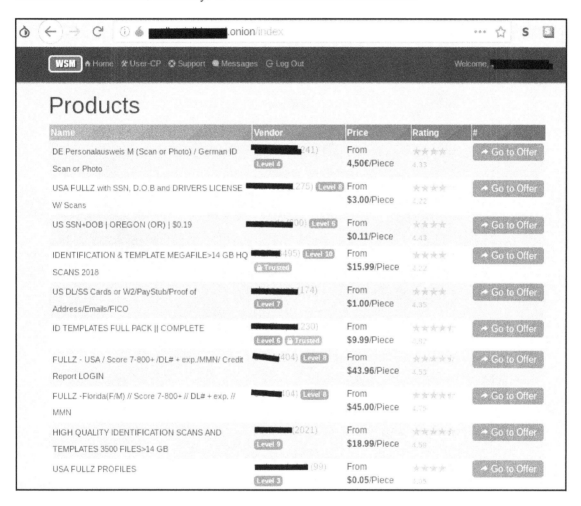

The following is a screenshot of the counterfeit documents available online:

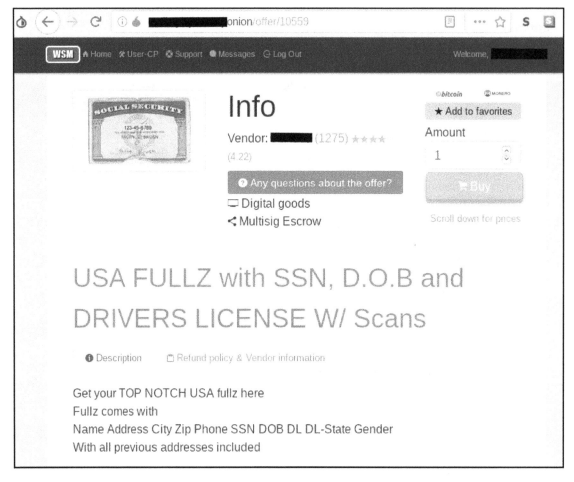

Counterfeit USA identification documents

Stolen information

Many sites are hacked, their information stolen, and then dumped on the Dark Web either for free, or to be purchased by the highest bidder, or a specific customer.

Today, there are many *dumps* of stolen data. Popular types of data are celebrity pictures, videos, and emails.

Hackers

In the past, hackers were considered dangerously highly-skilled professionals who should be kept at arm's length. Today, however, these individuals are sought after by enterprises, private companies, and nation states.

Black Hat Hackers are widespread on the Dark Web. These usually sell services, exploits, and tools on the Dark Web. They also use the Dark Web to communicate, plan attacks, and share exploits with each other.

Hacking services are very attractive on the Dark Web. Services offered by such hackers can be anything from performing a *realistic* penetration test to taking over a Facebook account. Such services are usually rendered at a cheap fee, which many can afford:

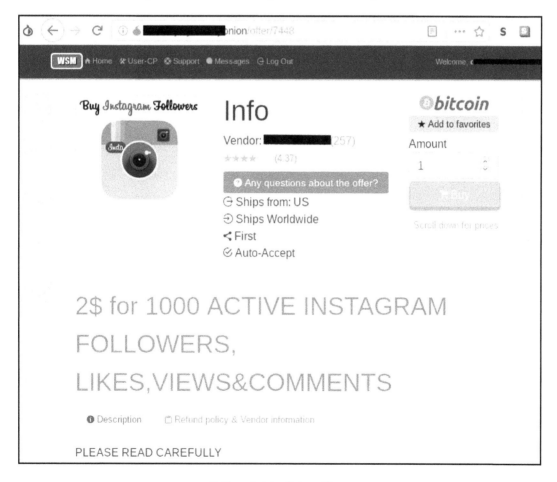

Hacking service to boost Instagram followers

The Dark Web holds a lot more than what was just described. There are sites that are dedicated to many beneficial or dangerous topics, such as hitmen for hire, killings, torture, and worse; or research, secure and anonymous communication, and more.

As you progress through this book, please be careful about how and what you access on the Dark Web, and do so at your own risk.

Read through the book before you go running to access the Dark Web, follow the explanations and recommendations, and always use Tor Browser, among other things.

Summary

In this chapter, we discussed what the internet is, what the Surface Web and the Deep Web are, what the Dark Web and darknets are, and observed several types of users of the Dark Web. We learned that in addition to being non-indexable, the Dark Web requires specialized software to access it.

In the following chapters, we'll discuss how to work with the Deep Web, and also discuss working with the Dark Web, a topic that we'll expand on as we go on in the book.

Questions

1. How would you label the three layers of the internet?

   A. Surface Web, Deep Web, internet

   B. Internet, Dark Net, Open Web

   C. Surface Web, Deep Web, Dark Web

   D. internet, Deep Web, Dark Net

2. What is responsible for indexing websites?

   A. Search engines

   B. Database servers

   C. Routers

   D. Bots

3. Organizations should exercise due diligence when storing privileged information on publicly accessible websites.

    A. True

    B. False

4. List three categories of data that are located on the deep web.

    A. Credit card information

    B. Private databases

    C. News headlines

    D. Academic journals

    E. Pictures hosted on Google Images

5. Name the components that make up the Dark Web.

    A. Darknets

    B. Firefox Incognito mode

    C. Overlay networks

    D. Content accessible using specialized software

6. Name two non-criminal uses of the Dark Web.

    A. Sale of counterfeit money

    B. Journalism

    C. Sale of an exploit tool you have developed

    D. Avoiding website tracking

7. Name two criminal uses of the Dark Web.

    A. Submitting a news article

    B. Obtaining a service to boost your Instagram followers

    C. Bypassing country censorships

    D. Buying counterfeit money

Further reading

The following resources might be interesting if you'd like to delve deeper into the topics included this chapter:

- https://www.internetsociety.org/internet/history-internet/brief-history-internet
- https://www.history.com/news/who-invented-the-internet
- https://en.wikipedia.org/wiki/Deep_web
- https://en.wikipedia.org/wiki/Dark_web

Working with the Deep Web 2

What goes on in the Dark Web? What can you do there?

In Chapter 9, *What Goes on in the Dark Web - Case Studies*, Chapter 10, *The Dangers of the Dark Web*, and Chapter 11, *Using the Dark Web for Your Business*, we will discuss case studies and stories of what goes on the Dark Web, and in this chapter, we'll discuss what you can do there. We'll talk about Dark web markets, and digital currency, browsing the Dark Web and more.

In this chapter we will cover the following topics:

- Maintaining privacy on the Dark Web
- Transacting on the Dark Web
- Deep web emails - Onion Mail

Maintaining privacy on the Dark Web

Privacy and anonymity are the underlying reasons for using the Dark Web, but why?

And how?

Privacy and anonymity are necessary for a functioning society. People want to feel safe and not monitored or investigated.

Even with the proliferation of social networks, and the oversharing of personal information there, many people still want to keep their data private, and to keep their personal information to themselves.

The internet provides a way to communicate and share, but as time goes by, its becoming a way for vendors to collect information about us to offer us products which are supposed to be what we want, according to our behavior on the network. It's also way for governments to monitor us, and a way for scam artists and criminals to collect information about us for their malicious intents.

Using the Dark web allows people to communicate, buy, connect and work privately and anonymously.

At least that's the idea. As with all technologies or environments, the less ethical among us utilize the advantages regarding anonymity and privacy that the Dark web provides, for their own ends.

Privacy can be defined as a state in which a person (or a corporate entity) can hide information about themselves from others. This can be done for various reasons, which ultimately doesn't matter. The idea is that, it's possible, or at least should be. This is becoming enforced by laws, such as GDPR, or any number of privacy acts and laws

Anonymity, can be described as hiding a person's true identity from others without hiding or censoring their activities.

As I've mentioned previously, the Internet has affected these terms, and lowered the level of both, for us.

Malicious hackers, companies and governments all collect information about us.

This harms our privacy. Few people understand how much.

Without privacy online, your information (personal or business) can be accessed and used, by the three types I listed previously (malicious hackers, companies, and governments).

Take advertising companies, for example. They collect information to be able to target us according to our preferences, search history, and other parameters, causing the effect we see, while surfing the Internet—receiving ads for products or services which we either searched for, took an interest in, or in some cases, accidentally clicked a link.

Governments collect this information to profile us and see if any person or group is a dissident, and to prevent crime or acts of terrorism. No matter what the reason is, they are invading our privacy.

It's important to understand that anonymity and privacy aren't the same.

You could be anonymous, but still not private, or vice versa. For most of us, our identity is our most precious asset, and many people prefer to have separate identities online, to ensure anonymity.

For some, anonymity is important to be able to voice their opinions without fear of retribution. For others, it's a matter of in which country they're located, and for others it depends on what their profession is.

Bottom line, we want to protect our information, be it medical, financial or personal. If a malicious hacker gains access to this information, we are at risk of theft, blackmail, impersonation, fraud, or any number of attacks that could harm us, in many ways.

Freedom of expression or speech is a right that must be exercised by all cultures and people

To preserve or maintain our online privacy and anonymity, we can use various tools, such as VPN's, Tor Browser, and by doing this, browse the Dark Web.

So how do we work in the Dark Web, while also maintaining our privacy and anonymity?

First, let's talk about what can be done on the Dark Web, focusing mainly on the legitimate uses.

Transacting on the Dark Web

To buy or sell on Dark Web markets, you need to understand a little about cryptocurrency. You've all probably heard about Bitcoin, which is the most well known one, but there are many others.

There are various ways to obtain Bitcoin or any other cryptocurrency, like purchasing or mining.

One of the important topics, transacting with cryptocurrency, is to maintain privacy. This is done by obfuscating the origin of bitcoins in a bitcoin wallet and the identity/location of the receiver.

This is usually performed by a 3rd party application/service, where the process can take between minutes to hours. Be careful when you look for one of these services, as there are scams in that market, usually due to the fact that they cost money, and provide vectors for scammers to steal our money.

Fraudulent sites pretend to be obfuscating services (also known as **tumblers**) and collect the money from unsuspecting users. The money will never reach the end target.

Always verify the service you want to work with for this (and in general), and use reputable services, which have existed for a qualified amount of time. Some Dark Web markets (AlphaBay, for example), offer these services for a small fee.

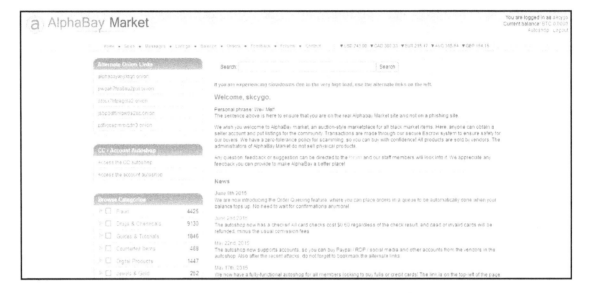

Secure transaction methods

There are three main cryptocurrency transaction methods:
Finalize Early (FE), Escrow and **Multiple Signature Escrow (multisig)**.

- **Finalize Early**: It is a payment method, in which a vendor requires receipt of payment before dispatching the purchased goods. The risk is on the buyer's end, but it also expedites the transaction due to little or no risk on the vendor's side (this method is the least secure for the buyer).
- **Escrow**: It is a payment method in which a Dark Web market will generate a bitcoin address to which the buyer transfers the payment. The market holds the buyer's money and pay's the vendor only after the buyer marks the order as complete. It is moderately secured.

- **Multiple Signature Escrow**: It is also called multisig, this payment method generates multiple keys for the bitcoin transaction and payment release process. The multisig can be either 2 out of 2 or 2 out of 3, where 2 of 3 provides the most security for three keys - the market's key, the vendor's key and the buyer's key. The keys are:
    - **2-of-2 Multisig**: Market public key, vendor public key
    - **2-of-3 Multisig**: Market public key, vendor public key + customer public key

After receiving the goods, the buyer signs off on the transaction using his/her key, and then the market uses their key and releases the funds to the vendor.

If there are any issues, lack of communication, or if the buyer doesn't approve receival of goods, the market can mediate the transaction and use its key which is highly secure.

Another part of financial transactions on the Dark Web are blockchains. As I've mentioned in a Chapter 9, *What Goes on in the Dark Web - Case Studies*, blockchain is a public ledger in which all virtual transactions are indexed and recorded. Hackers can create **orphaned blocks**, through which they can attempt to take complete control of the blockchain ledger by manipulating the blocks in the ledger. There was a comparatively known attack, called the **51% attack**.

Always try to use the most secure option when performing transactions on the Dark Web.

I mentioned that there are several ways to obtain Bitcoin. One is buying Bitcoin from confirmed vendors, the other is Bitcoin Mining. This is done by individuals or groups, using dedicated hardware, which compiles a few hundred transactions from the blockchain ledger and then turns them into a mathematical problem.

Solving these problems results in new Bitcoin for the **miners**, referred to as **block reward** and verification of the Bitcoin payment network.

Bitcoin, or any other cryptocurrency (or even traditional currency) is always at risk from scams or frauds. One of the frauds that I've heard about, is related to "Bitcoin mining hardware".
Scammers pose as legitimate hardware manufacturers, specializing in Bitcoin mining hardware, and collect money from people to develop or manufacture *new and special* Bitcoin mining systems, naturally never returning on investment and vanishing with the money.

Here are a few things to keep in mind while browsing the Dark Web:

- So if you want to make purchases on the Dark Web markets, remember—vet the market site first. Make sure it's not a scam.
- Second—never use your debit/credit card on a Dark Web site, never use Paypal, and if you purchase Bitcoin, do it from a legitimate seller who offers escrow services, or mine for Bitcoin. It's not that fast, or simple, but is feasible.
- Another common use for the Dark Web is browsing, and searching for content that either costs money on the Surface Web or that you can't find the information due to its sensitive or illicit nature.
- Always exercise common sense while browsing the Dark Web.
  Beware if people act too friendly, or if something seems too good to be true. Remember that people might try to take advantage of your fears of the Dark Web, when most of your fears aren't true, but are based on stories.
- Always use Tor Browser and preferably a VPN, before browsing to a Dark Web site, additionally, after finishing this book, you'll be able to decide which operating system to use when you connect to the Dark Web (Do Not use Windows).
- One of them, **Tails**, boots your machine from a USB flash drive, which helps the privacy and security of the user. This is good since nothing will remain on the computer when you reboot.

As I will discuss in `Chapter 5`, *Accessing the Dark Web with Tor Browser*, you can browse to the Dark Web version of Facebook, which was created to provide access to Facebook, in countries where it's blocked on the Surface Web. You can join online clubs and gaming groups, and basically do almost everything you might do on the Surface Web, just more cautiously.

Searching for information is not always as easy as Googling. But you can use Dark Web search engines, or rather indexes which will take you to the relevant sites, for example **Torch**:

TORCH search engine

Ahmia, is another Dark Web search engine , which blacklists any inappropriate or invalid data:

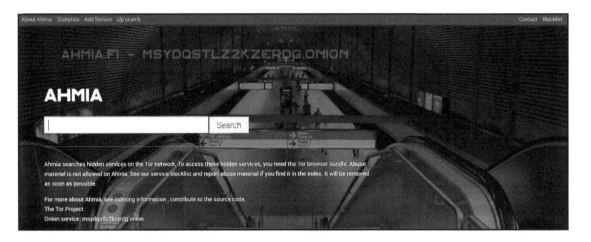

In the next screenshot, you'll be able to see another Dark Web search engine—**notEvil**.

notEvil search engine of Dark Web

DuckDuckGo is one of the most famous search engines, also used for searching on the Surface Web, since it doesn't retain search history or any other user activity.

Tor Links is a source for dark web links. Tor Links is user-friendly and organized. Drugs, digital goods, erotic, gambling, hacking, forums, media and more can be found here.

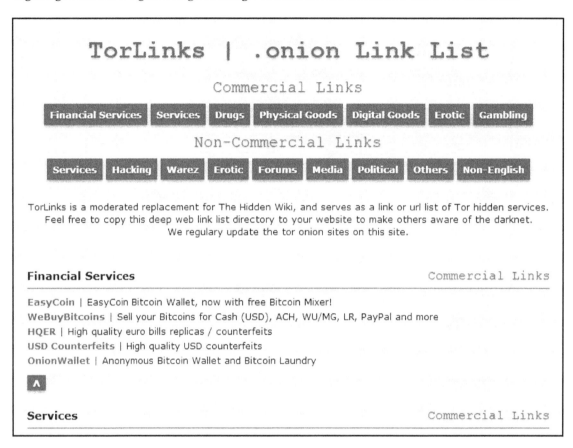

The same as on the Surface Web there are multiple anonymous mail services. Some of them are:

- **Scryptmail**. It is free for 7 days and can be accessed on the Surface Web as well:

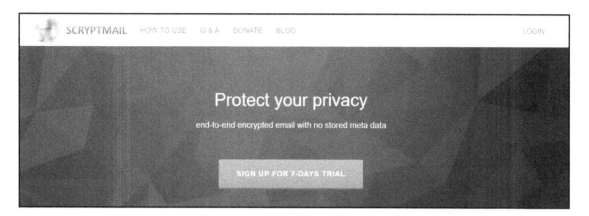

- **Bitmessage Mail Gateway**: It has Auto responder, Auto forwarder, broadcasting, two auto signatures and many more. Also, it is completely free.

Register | Setup Guide | FAQ | E-Mail access | E-Mail settings | Terms and conditions | TOR access

Bitmessage Mail Gateway

This is a service to connect Bitmessage with E-Mail without the need of any software
It allows you to use the Bitmessage network the same way you use E-Mail today.

Key Features

- It's completely free
- No advertisments anywhere
- No tracking with Google Analytics or other services at all
- Send and receive E-Mails from/to Bitmessage addresses
- Send and receive E-Mails from/to other E-Mail addresses
- Personal Bitmessage address
- Supports broadcasting
- Use the E-Mail client you are satisfied with and all its features (address book, spam filter, folders, rules, etc).
- Instant delivery (no **POW**) if your contact has an @bitmessage.ch address too.
- Server supports IMAP, POP3 and SMTP
- Easy readable alias address
- No Proxy or TOR required but TOR hidden service available (see **FAQ**)
- Webmail Access from everywhere.
- Two webmail systems, one optimized for bitmessage compatibility, one for all E-Mail features (attachments, MIME, ...)
- Auto responder if you are away or want to set up a mailing list.
- Auto forwarder to an external address.
- Two auto signatures (Plain Text and HTML).
- Rules for automatic message filtering.

Deep web emails - Onion Mail

Onion Mail is another working anonymous email service provider at hidden web.

To create a new Onion Mail account, you need to click on **Download** option and then you will notice another window with a message **To create a new OnionMail account click HERE**. For more info about Onion Mail features and services, please visit Tor URL: (`http://it.louhlbgyupgktsw7.onion/`).

CryptoDog is a private chat server on the Dark Web:

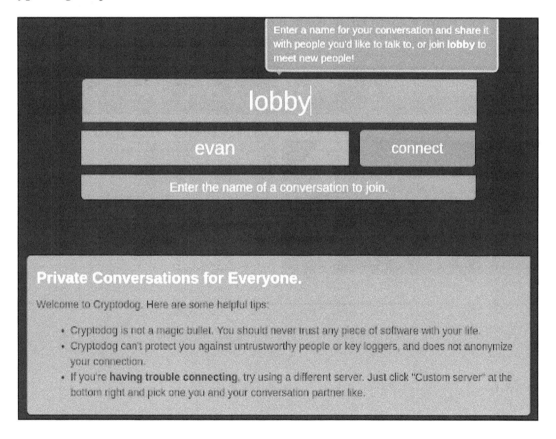

There are also many forums sites on the Dark Web, for example:

- Anonymous Forum
- Pedo Support Community
- Glazy2
- 8Chan
- Nnptchan
- HiddenChan

DeepDotWeb is a blog which covers the latest deep web news and other useful tutorials like how to buy drugs online, PGP tutorials, how to access dark web links, and more:

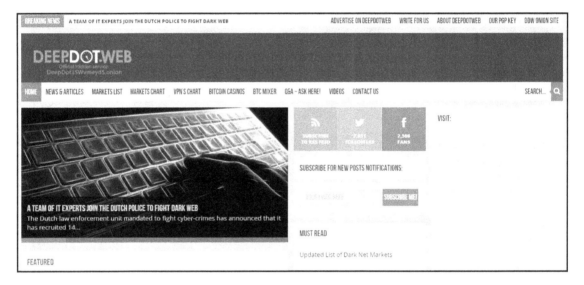

Wikileaks is the infamous news leak site:

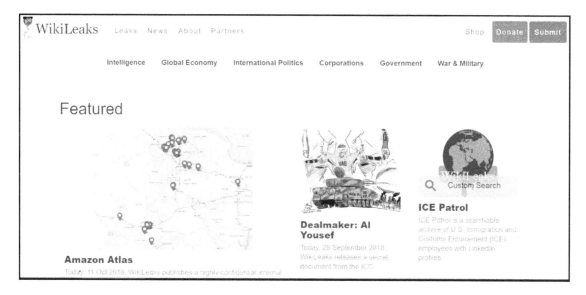

SoylentNews has content regarding multiple topics:

BitStore and Mobile Store sell mobile phones and related products.

Electronion or Electron shop are sites which offer electronic gadgets for sale.

Summary

The Dark Web has many uses. Some of them are benign and some are malevolent.

Part of the goal of this book is to expose you to them, so you will be better prepared and will be able to avoid problems or prevent them.

The important thing to remember is that you just need to be careful, take the precautions I will tell you about, and *keep your eyes open*.

Questions

1. Please describe what Privacy and Anonymity are.
2. What are the 3 main cryptocurrency transaction methods?
3. Please list 3 Dark Web search websites.
4. What uses are there for the Dark Web?
    1. Browsing
    2. Email
    3. Blogging
    4. Forums
    5. Financial Transacting
    6. Almost everything you might do on the Surface Web (including all the above)

Further reading

The following resources might be interesting if you'd like to delve deeper into the topics included this chapter:

- `https://www.thedarkweblinks.com/`
- `https://computer.howstuffworks.com/internet/basics/how-the-deep-web-works.htm`

The Future of the Dark Web 3

In the following chapters, we'll discuss the technical side of accessing the Dark Web.

When I start using any technology, I try to think what it will look like in the future. How it will be used, how it will develop, and who will be using it.

In this chapter, we'll try to address these questions, talking less about the buzz you hear about, such as illegal activity, but rather focusing on the future of the positive and practical aspects, such as online markets, and, more importantly, privacy. For the future of the Dark Web is intrinsically entwined with the future of privacy for all of us.

So let's go...back to the future!

We will cover the following topics in this chapter:

- What does the future of the Deep Web hold for us
- Dark Web markets
- The TOR Project
- Public interest in the Dark Web

What does the future of the Deep Web hold for us?

To contemplate the future of the Dark Web, we need to also discuss the Deep Web, since they are intrinsically related. As I explained in `Chapter 1`, *Understanding the Deep and Dark Web*, the Dark Web is a sub-section of the Deep Web. The future is almost always unclear, especially regarding technology, which progresses in leaps and bounds, and is usually, not in a linear fashion.

If you remember, the Deep Web's difference from the Surface (WWW) Web is the fact that the sites and content there aren't crawled or indexed, so won't be accessible via standard search browsers.

Organizational content and intranets are part of the Deep Web, but more and more of them are being relocated from on-premise solutions, to cloud-based environments, such as AWS, Azure, and Google Cloud. There is a concern among users of these technologies that the vendors are collecting information about them.

For example, Google has talked about non-stop collection of data, both private and otherwise. This is probably true regarding all search engines and/or hosting companies, so there will be changes in how organizations and people access the Deep Web.

These changes will include how they authenticate (biometrics, voice, 2FA, and more), how they access the Deep Web, and more.

But, ultimately, many sites, services, and users will change the way they access Deep Web content.

And what about the Dark Web, you might ask?

According to forecasts, the Dark Web will be become more mainstream, yet harder to breach.

The UI of applications designed to access the Dark Web, such as Tor, are becoming more user friendly, helping the mainstream trend.

Dark Web currency

Dark Web currency (that is, Bitcoin, and so on), will grow, with many more cryptocurrencies popping up, which will also be a result (or the cause) of a proliferation of Dark Web access.

In the future, there will be new, completely decentralized marketplaces that rely on Bitcoin's (or a different cryptocurrency's) blockchain technology. This technology will apparently be used to guarantee trust between buyers and sellers and to ensure safe transactions.

Currently, the top cryptocurrencies are Ripple, Litecoin, Ethereum, Dash, Dogecoin, Banxshares, Stellar, BitShares, Bytecoin, and Nxt, with more popping up all the time.

The following screenshots taken from several cryptocurrency websites.

Ethereum is a decentralized platform that runs on a custom built blockchain, an enormously powerful shared global infrastructure that can move value around and represent the ownership of property. You could look at it as a secure cryptocurrency platform. Let's look at the following screenshot:

Ripple is a company that provides a secure blockchain-based network, to facilitate secure transactions, called RippleNet. Let's look at the following screenshot:

Litecoin is a peer-to-peer online currency. It's an open source, global payment network that is fully decentralized without any central authorities. Litecoin is a proven medium of commerce complementary to Bitcoin. Let's look at the following screenshot:

Dark Web markets

Since the operations leading to the closing of Dark Web markets, and the ensuing trials, are a matter of public record, many hundreds of people think of new ways to work and create new markets that are harder to bring down.

It's also important to remember that many of these markets sell legitimate goods or services, where the illegal part is usually a lack of taxation on the sale of goods, or a lack of documentation as vendors, and other bureaucratic reasons. Take Dr.X as an example—he provides medical advice, testing of recreational drugs, and support for recreational drug users. There are many countries in the world where this is a legal and positive service.

You can even find vegetables, electronics, and a multitude of other goods that are quite legal to buy and sell.

The original goal of Dark Web markets was to provide free marketplaces, without censorship, where prices are fair and there's no *middle man* between the vendor/seller and the buyer; where the market or the vendor doesn't collect information about us.

Many *regular* market sites advocate information gathering to help with *personalizing* the products offered to us.

Personally, I greatly prefer to search by myself, and not receive offers or have product advertisements sent to me, but nowadays marketing works like that.

The Dark Web markets of the future (and of today, actually) won't collect information about us, unless we allow it. That's just how the Dark Web works.

Think about it: you access a market site, search for what you want, without receiving suggestions or offers, based on your previous purchases, since the market doesn't collect anything about you. I know that I would like that.

Until recently, Dark Web markets came and went. Usually, they were closed by law enforcement, while other times hackers brought them down.

For example, Agora, one of the top markets in 2015, was shut down, due to attempts to crack their security defenses (it is unknown if they shut down themselves or were forced to shut down)

Other markets, such as Hansa and Silk Road Reloaded, expanded their trading onto I2P channels, where they compete with more traditional marketplaces., such as OpenBazaar, a Bitcoin-based market that offers an inventory of goods and services on the Surface Web. Their framework allows for trading directly with customers, using the **Invisible Internet Project** (**I2P**) network, multisig addresses (multisig addresses require multiple keys to authorize a Bitcoin transaction, which allows for dividing up possession of bitcoins), and digital signatures to provide secure communication directly between the buyer and seller.

This is what was displayed on the Hansa site, after it was closed:

Screenshot of Hansa site

In May 2017, OpenBazaar incorporated a Tor mode option that allows users to become a relay, as part of a Tor network. This will effectively obscure and protect their identity, making OpenBazaar a form of a Dark net site. Since the creators of OpenBazaar view their market as an anonymous one, it is possible for sales of illegal goods to happen, but if this has or will happen, only time will tell.

Anonymous marketplace-based trading will expand and become mainstream in the future. Many questions exist, such as how to resolve differences between anonymous entities (buyer and seller), how to prevent scamming, and more.

How they will be resolved remains to be seen.

The following screenshot shows the homepage of OpenBazaar:

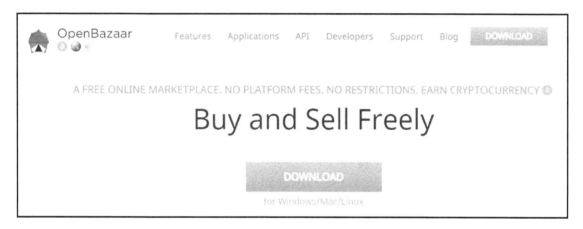

Homepage of OpenBazaar

The following screenshot displays FAQs from the OpenBazaar site, explaining its concept:

Frequently Asked Questions

What is OpenBazaar?

OpenBazaar is a different way to do online commerce. It's a peer to peer application that doesn't require middlemen, which means no fees & no restrictions.

How does OpenBazaar work?

OpenBazaar connects people directly via a peer to peer network. Data is distributed across the network instead of storing it in a central database.

How are there no fees and restrictions?

OpenBazaar isn't a company nor an organization; it's free open source software. It was built to provide everyone with the ability to buy and sell freely

Who controls the OpenBazaar network?

Nobody has control over OpenBazaar. Each user contributes to the network equally and is in control of their own store and private data

Is Bitcoin the only supported payment method?

Pay with 50+ cryptocurrencies on OpenBazaar: Bitcoin, Ethereum, Litecoin, Zcash, Dash, etc. Seller receives payment in Bitcoin, Bitcoin Cash or Zcash. Their choice.

A proposed solution for these Dark Web markets is decentralization. It can help with issues of market operator trust. It provides peer-to-peer sites, written in open source code (more secure), high level of encryption, and privacy.

Centralization is an issue on the Surface Web. Huge companies control large portions of the internet real estate. Take Google, Amazon, and Microsoft, for example. Can we really trust them with our privacy? Let's hope so.

Blockchain behavior should also be implemented into these marketplaces in the future.

One instance where decentralization was tried was Pirate Bay. In 2014, they planned to implement a decentralized version of their site, which would use the resources of the user's machine (buyer or seller). This would ensure continuity of the site, and continue, as long as users accessed it.

This didn't happen in the end, but the idea was sound, and can be implemented in the future.

ZeroNet:

ZeroNet has created a peer-to-peer system, preventing censorship and hosting costs, without a single point of failure.

ZeroNet removes IP addresses and assigns cryptographic keys to websites, similar to a cryptocurrency wallet address. The public key is the site address, and the private key gives the key holder the ability to create and maintain the site. Users provide the sites to each other, as peers.

The following screenshot of what ZeroNet say about itself is taken from its website:

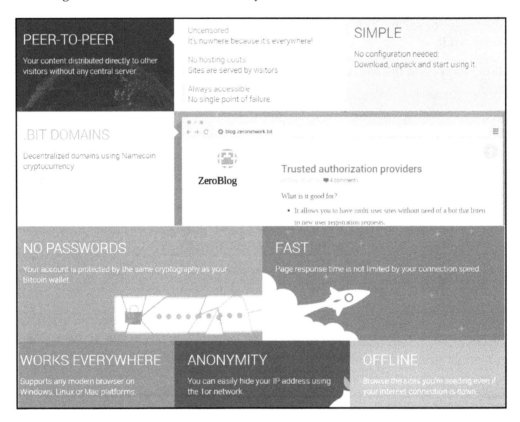

ZeroBazaar is an example of a new project, a combination of ZeroNet and OpenBazaar, utilizing the best of both technologies, and providing a truly free and private online market.

The TOR Project

As we will discuss in detail in a different chapter, one of the ways to connect to the Dark Web is by using the Tor Browser. It allows a user to connect to the Tor network one of the major Dark nets out there.

As we'll discuss, even without connecting to the Tor network, the Tor Browser provides anonymity and privacy while surfing Surface Web websites.

Due to the rising importance of privacy, the Tor Project is focusing even more on this and on security.

One of the main improvements allows users to host websites anonymously and privately.

Tor's anonymity is based on relays—random computers (also referred to as routers or nodes) between which communication is bounced, to obfuscate the route through which communication is performed, effectively hiding the source and destination addresses, and safeguarding their privacy.

The problem arises from weaknesses (vulnerabilities) inherent in Tor, the same as you may find in any software or technology.

For example, if attackers have control over enough nodes within the Tor network, then they can see both the entry point node and the exit node. They will be able to detect the source of the request and don't need to know what happens in between.

They then modify the headers of the packets in the entry nodes and if they find those packets on the exit nodes they control, they will be able to connect the packets to someone. These types of attacks are called traffic confirmation attacks.

Tor addresses these problems by upgrading the onion services feature.

Onion services allow users to operate a website, chat service, file sharing site, or video-calling platform without exposing their IP address. This feature allows users to run onion services from behind firewalls.

The upgrade will resolve a number of flaws that have existed since the original design of onion services.

For example, in the past, a Tor user was able to set up an onion service manually or by using third-party programs, such as Onionshare. To make the services known, something only the creator could do, he would have to make the services known manually.

Another of those Tor vulnerabilities allows attackers to discover the services, since they had to broadcast their existence to a number of Tor relays.

If an attacker got control of enough relays to identify new onion service registrations, they could develop an index of public and private onion sites, and then replace onion service relays, making the original services unreachable, effectively taking sites offline.

An additional results of the upgrade is that the network will randomly assign the relays that each onion service contacts. The relay message will also be encrypted, making it unreadable to the human operator, but the relay will automatically follow the command.

Also, the onion domain names will include more characters.

Once, they were made up of 16 randomly generated characters. Now they will have 56 random characters.

These improvements should make it much more difficult to discover private (hidden) onion services. And if they are discovered, they require a password. Also, the RSA cryptosystem is being replaced by a more efficient elliptic-curve cryptography.

The hash functions and secret keys for the Advanced Encryption Standard are also upgraded. These improvements are not only aimed at current users, but intend to draw new users to use Tor

Also, as more regular users are using Tor for ethical and legal reasons, the appearance of publicly broadcasted onion services is growing, providing more trustworthy services.

The following screenshot shows the improvements in the latest version of Tor (December 2018):

New Release: Tor Browser 8.0.4

by gk | December 11, 2018

Tor Browser 8.0.4 is now available from the Tor Browser Project page and also from our distribution directory.

Tor Browser 8.0.4 contains updates to Tor (0.3.4.9), OpenSSL (1.0.2q) and other bundle components. Additionally, we backported a number of patches from our alpha series where they got some baking time. The most important ones are

- a defense against protocol handler enumeration which should enhance our fingerprinting resistance,
- enabling Stylo for macOS users by bypassing a reproducibility issue caused by Rust compilation and
- setting back the sandboxing level to 5 on Windows (the Firefox default), after working around some Tor Launcher interference causing a broken Tor Browser experience.

Moreover, we ship an updated donation banner for our year-end donation campaign.

The full changelog since Tor Browser 8.0.3 is:

- All platforms
  - Update Firefox to 60.4.0esr
  - Update Tor to 0.3.4.9
  - Update OpenSSL to 1.0.2q
  - Update Torbutton to 2.0.9
    - Bug 28540: Use new text for 2018 donation banner
    - Bug 28515: Use en-US for english Torbutton strings
    - Translations update
  - Update HTTPS Everywhere to 2018.10.31
  - Update NoScript to 10.2.0
  - Bug 1623: Block protocol handler enumeration (backport of fix for #680300)
  - Bug 25794: Disable pointer events
  - Bug 26608: Disable background HTTP response throttling
  - Bug 28165: Add smallerRichard to Tor Browser
- Windows
  - Bug 26381: about:tor page does not load on first start on Windows
  - Bug 28657: Remove broken FTE bridge from Tor Browser
- OS X
  - Bug 26475: Fix Stylo related reproducibility issue
  - Bug 26263: App icon positioned incorrectly in macOS DMG installer window

Public interest in the Dark Web

The public interest in the Dark Web is growing, especially among *regular* users. These include everyday people like you or me, who aren't criminals, but are extremely interested in the Dark Web, due to the overload of content that we get from the media.

TV shows (*Mr. Robot*, *CSI:Cyber*, *Black Mirror*, to name a few), movies, books, documentaries, and every form of media have been covering the Dark Web in the past few years, and it looks like the trend will only continue.

On the news, we hear about massive hacks (Facebook, British Airways, Ashley Madison, and others) where the data stolen is offered on the Dark Web to the highest bidder.

This image was displayed by British Airways, following their hack:

All these have made even the most technophobic individuals interested in accessing the Dark Web, just to *take a peek* at what they hear about.

As we move forward in this book, you'll realize that there's not that much of a difference between the Surface Web and the Dark Web, except for two main factors—the technological one: the requirement to use specific software to access content there, and the philosophical one—anonymity and privacy abounds there, which simply makes it easier for the criminal elements to perform their activities without revealing who they are.

That's the main reason why illicit activities are more pronounced or readily available for viewing on the Dark Web.
But as we've discussed, and will continue to discuss, taking the proper precautions to protect your anonymity and your security will provide a user experience very similar to what you usually experience on the Surface Web.

Private delivery services will provide untraceable, secure, and anonymous delivery.

One of the things that many people dislike is the way that most regular delivery services invade their privacy. The goal of these delivery companies will be to provide autonomous and anonymous drones, invisible to street-cams, radar, and infrared scanners, delivering packages, payed in cryptocurrency, with no logs of the deliveries.

Yes, this can be used for delivery of illegal products, but one proposed safety mechanism would be detecting bombs or other weapons of mass destruction, and only delivering objects that aren't publicly dangerous. I expect this to be something that will gain focus, since sending such objects, which might result in harm to others, would be a liability to these delivery services, and would harm their reputation and income from the non-criminal market. But, as we are talking about the future, let's wait and see.

One of the problems on the Dark Web is the lack of a justice system. There is no organization that moderates or is supposed to prevent wrong-doing. Of course, there's a very fine line between what's wrong and right on the Dark Web, but it can be agreed that the original intent of the Dark Web is to enhance anonymity and privacy, and not to condone crime. Having said that, many experts agree that actions that harm the privacy and anonymity of an individual or of a business entity should be prevented, in addition to scams and theft, ensuring honest trading (buy/sell anonymously and don't cheat the other side). Sadly, reality is a little different, and people of a less than sterling nature will always try to take advantage of others and do what they want without consideration of morality.

Thankfully, there's an evolution of a Dark Web justice system, which according to the signs, will be a peer justice system, with the majority of users deciding how to resolve conflicts and how to penalize wrong-doers.

Summary

Privacy is becoming more and more important, as there are almost unlimited ways in which information is being collected about us. In some areas, it's regulated in some manner (GDPR in the EU, for example), in others, privacy is non-existent.

The UN has tried to standardize human rights, including the right to privacy (Article 12 of the Universal Declaration of Human Rights).

The following screenshot displays the UN site with the declaration:

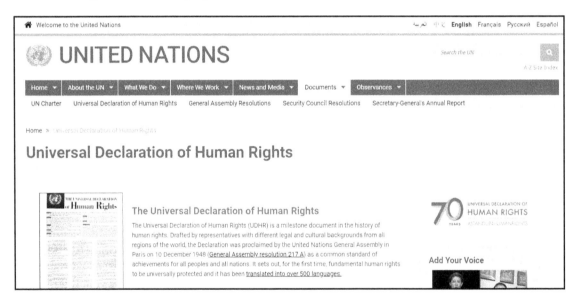

The Dark Web is the great equalizer. A way to go online without giving up on our privacy.

It is the beginning of a revolution that will put our privacy at its center.

So in the future, more and more people will use it, to be able to communicate, consume content, purchase or sell goods, and more, with a high level of anonymity.

In the future, the Dark Web will be *the* anonymous communication medium.

Look out for it.

Questions

1. Name three improvements in Tor.
2. Name at least three Dark Web markets.
3. What are the main proposed future changes in the Dark Web?

4

Installing a Linux Virtual
Machine (VM)

In the previous chapter, we discussed what the future of the Dark Web might be. As you may know, there are various operating systems on the market. Windows, macOS, ChromeOS, and Linux are the most common (not necessarily in that order). The operating system which is the most secure, and the one which we'll be using for several chapters, is Linux.

Linux has many flavors (distros), which we'll discuss in this chapter, including how to install them (we'll talk about one, but the idea is the same for most of them).

Let's start getting our hands dirty by installing Linux, the Tor browser, and accessing the Dark Web.

In this chapter, we will cover the following topics:

- Linux Distributions
- Installing and using a Linux VM
- What else can we do with a Linux VM?

Linux Distributions

Red Hat, Fedora, Ubuntu, and CentOS are just a few of the more common Linux distributions out there that you can use for everyday use or, in the context of this book, to install the Tor browser on it and access the Deep Web.

The levels of privacy and anonymity you want to reach are the main factors in choosing an OS for Deep Web browsing. There are several security-dedicated Linux-based OSes out there, which we will discuss later in the book.

For now, let's talk a little about Linux (and what a distribution is).

Linux was developed by Linus Torvalds, a Finnish computer science student, in 1991. In those days, Unix-like systems were the craze, but they were either incompatible with most PCs, or too expensive.

Linux started as a program, specifically for use with Torvalds' personal 80386 PC, but, as time went on, it evolved into an OS.

I won't go into the details of the evolution of Linux, but I will mention several important aspects of the OS:

- First, it's free
- It's also free to distribute and share
- It's also pretty secure, stable, and reliable
- Linux is also very customizable, especially if you're a coder

Since Linux is so open, there are many different versions, each of them slightly different from the others. These versions are called distributions, or distros, for short.

Before we install a Linux distribution, the question arises—which one is the best for me?

Well, since there are so many distributions, it is a matter of preference and what you want to achieve with the OS. Some distribution have more emphasis on the desktop user interface, while others are server versions, and others still are focused on security (both defensive and offensive).

A few of the more common desktop Linux distributions are Ubuntu, Mint, Fedora, Debian, and openSUSE. Several of the common server Linux distributions are Red Hat Enterprise Linux, Ubuntu Server, CentOS, and SUSE Enterprise Linux. We will start with a *standard* Linux distribution, and as we move through the book, we will examine several of the best Linux-based OSes for accessing the Deep Web.

Before you install any OS- Linux or any other- operating system, read up about it, what its weaknesses and fortes are, and most importantly, what resources are required to install it.

Linux has several advantages over Windows and even macOS, which tend to make it more secure, but as with any technology, how you use it can also affect its security.

The first advantage is that, by default, users created in Linux do not have administrative privileges. Of course, the user can change this, but if used correctly, remaining with the default privileges is a great security advantage.

Running or installing applications requires the elevation of privileges, which means that most Malware, Trojans, Backdoors, and so on will not be able to execute on download.

The fact that the vast majority of the world uses Windows is also an advantage—most hacks are pointed to that OS, which means that there are less pointed at Linux.

In addition, the diversity of Linux distribution means that each Linux OS is slightly different, which means that hackers usually need to develop specific exploits for each one. The fact that most of the OSes are Windows means that there are less ready-made hacks out there, compared to Linux.

Since Linux is free and its source code is also freely available, countless people review its source code and find any flaws or weaknesses, fix them, and then redistribute the improved code.

The sheer number of tester-users means that, statistically, most of the security flaws (and other types of flaws) will be detected and fixed, and in a comparatively short time. With Windows, mainly Microsoft employees find these flaws, meaning that there is a much smaller group of people working to find issues, and thus fewer issues are found, before the OS is released.

I will elaborate on best practices for accessing the Deep Web in a different chapter, but in general, the most important factors you need to consider are as follows:

- Use a VPN. The VPN you choose should have the following features: be able to connect via other countries' servers, prevent IP or DNS leaks, and have a kill switch if your VPN goes down.
- Use Tor to access the Dark Web, to minimize your exposure.

Let's explain some of the terms I just mentioned:

- IP leaks occur when your browser reveals your computer's IP address, even when connected to a VPN. This can be prevented by using VPNs that are designed to prevent IP leaks.
- DNS leaks occur when your computer forwards its DNS request to your ISP's DNS server rather than through the VPN you are using.

These two types of leaks occur due to weaknesses that exist in the computer's browser or OS.

A kill switch is a mechanism built into some VPNs that disconnects the internet connection of the computer, when the VPN disconnects unexpectedly, rather than returning to the default configuration of your computer, as supplied by your ISP. Without a kill switch, your computer will switch back to the ISP connection, exposing you to the public:

- Use the Tor browser. First, you won't be able to access Deep Web sites without it. But, it's also important to minimize your risks. We'll discuss Tor in the next chapter.
- Practice basic precautions, such as never using your real name, never giving out your passwords, bank, or credit card information, and so on, while on the Deep Web.

Also, always use complex passwords or passphrases, cover your camera, and if possible, disable your microphone.

I will go into more detail in the chapter regarding best practices for accessing the Deep Web.

Installing and using a Linux VM

Here, we will be installing Ubuntu.

According to the `www.ubuntu.com` website, the required resources to install Ubuntu Desktop Edition are as follows:

- 2 GHz dual core processor
- 2 GB RAM (system memory)
- 25 GB of hard-drive space (Ubuntu can also be installed on a USB stick, memory card, or external drive)
- A monitor capable of 1024x768 screen resolution

I installed Ubuntu on a VM, but the process is the same on a PC.

For those of you that don't know what a VM is, you could say that it's a virtual computer, run by specialized software, either on your desktop or in a dedicated environment. These virtual computers are called *guests*, and they are run on a *host* OS.

I personally use VMware Workstation, but there are several out there, depending on your host OS and specific requirements.

As with most OSes, Linux can be installed from a DVD, an ISO file, or a USB flash drive. Some people even prefer running their entire OS from a USB flash drive, for enhanced security.

To install Linux from a USB flash drive, you will need software taht will make the USB stick bootable.

There are many tools you can use, and you should try several until you find one that you feel comfortable with.

I use Universal USB Installer, which is a free utility, under the GNU general public license.

To get back to our Linux installation, let's go over the general steps:

1. Obtain Linux installation media (an ISO file, for example). You can obtain one by performing a web search for any distribution you want.
2. Read the installation requirements.
3. Prepare the machine you will be installing on, either VM or physical, according to the installation requirements.
4. Install from a USB flash drive, DVD, or ISO file.

Now that we have talked about the basics, let's get started.

I prepared a VM, with the required specifications, and even added more resources, to make the installed OS more efficient (and faster), as you can see here:

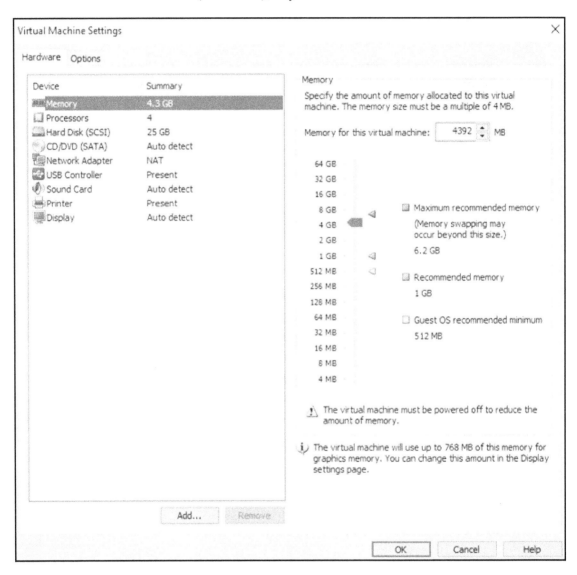

VM settings

As soon as your PC or VM boots, you will see the following on your screen:

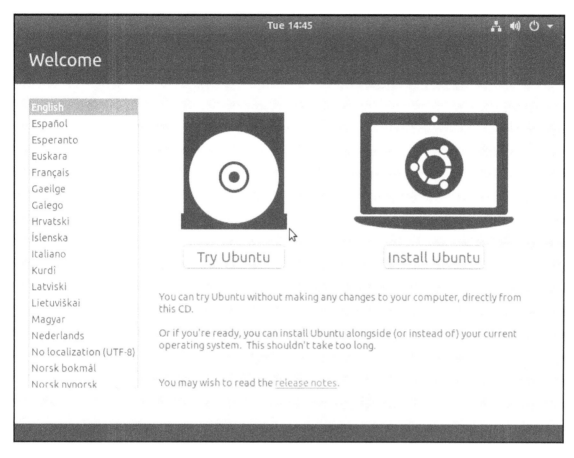

Ubuntu installation Welcome screen

Choose the language you want, and then click **Install Ubuntu**.

Another option is to boot from the CD/DVD/USB flash drive, if you click **Try Ubuntu**.

Next, you will see a screen with options for choosing your keyboard layout:

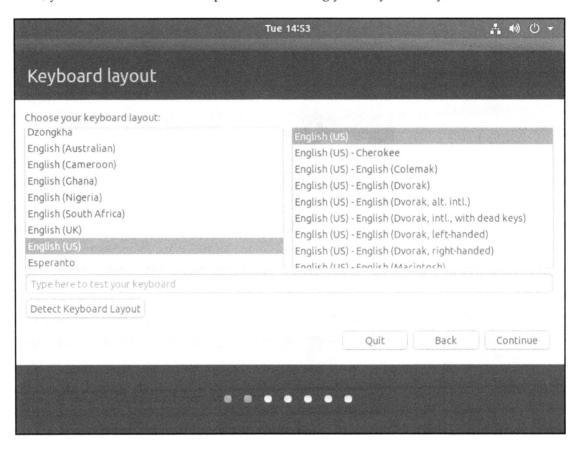

Ubuntu Keyboard layout choice screen

The next screen is for deciding whether to install the default apps and other software that you want available from the start:

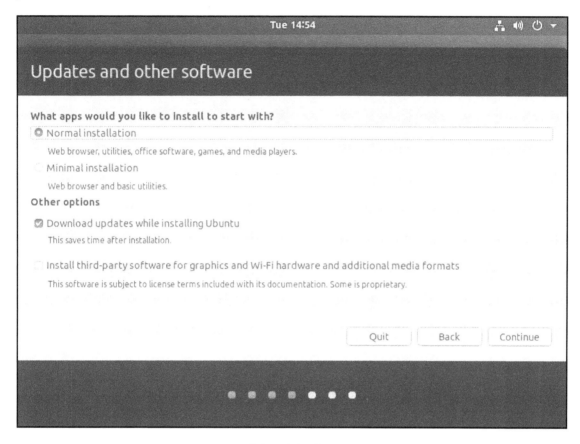

Updates and other software

The **Installation type** screen allows you to decide whether to delete any previous OSes you may have installed on the same computer, and provides the option to encrypt the new OS, and to use **Logical Volume Management** (**LVM**), for easy partition resizing and management:

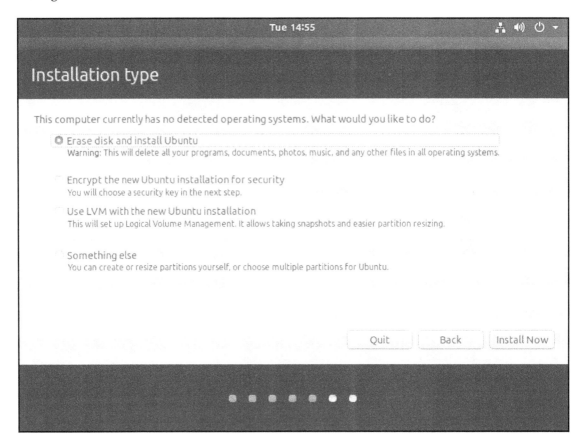

The **Where are you?** screen is basically for setting your time zone:

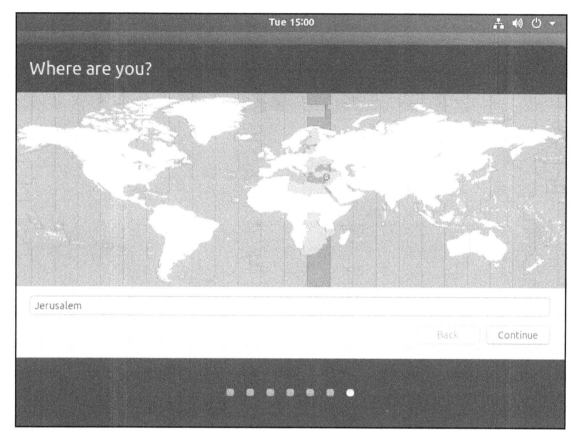

Where are you?

The **Who are you?** screen is where you provide your name (or the name that you want listed in the OS) the computer's name, a username, and a password.

Remember that you will probably use this installation to access the Deep Web. Use a handle or pseudonym in any OS you use for that purpose, for all the names you use:

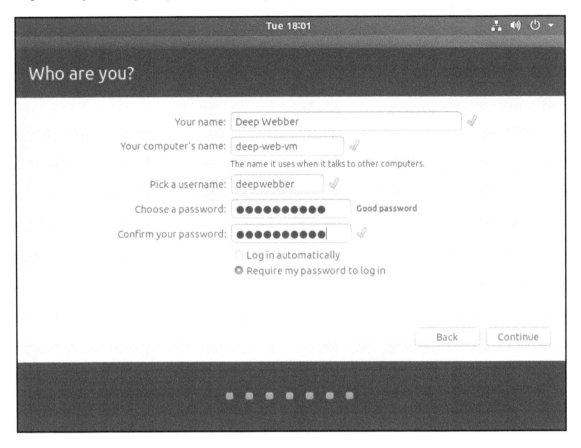

Then, you'll see the installation process occur. This can take anywhere between a few minutes and an hour.

The final screen will tell you that the installation is complete, and you'll have to restart to be able to use the new installation. Do so by clicking **Restart Now**.

After the installation completes, the computer will reboot, after which, you'll reach the login screen, as displayed here:

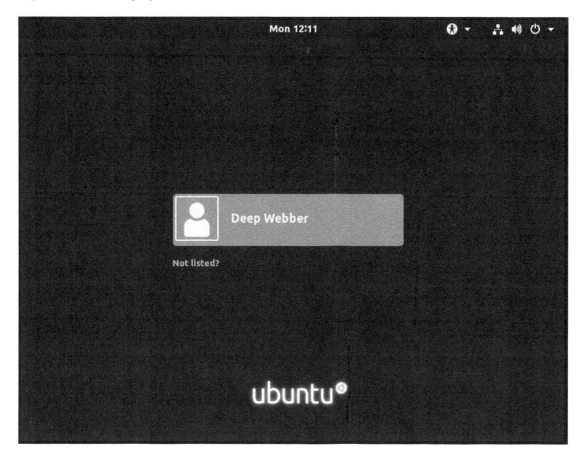

Clicking on the username will display the login box. Enter your password and click **Sign in** or press *Enter*:

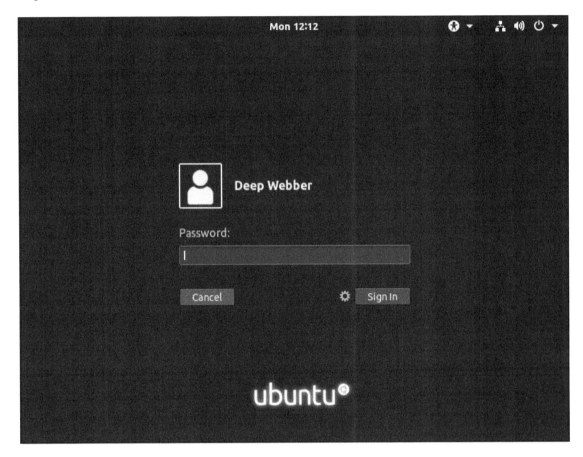

What else can we do with a Linux VM?

Now that we've installed Linux, what do we do with it?

Well, the obvious answer is install Tor browser. Yes, but that's in the next chapter. First, let's familiarize ourselves with Linux a bit.

Linux has the same basic functions as Windows—browsers, apps, OpenOffice for a productivity suite, a desktop interface, and so on, but there are so many more things you can do with Linux as an OS, from using it to run a smart home, a media center, and more.

You can completely customize Linux, by changing things such as the desktop environment, and can even customize the OS and the applications, if you're a coder, or if you develop your coding skills.

Programming is easier with Linux, with its built-in apps that can help you to read and write code. Accessing the log files of the OS, or anything you develop, is much easier with Linux, as well.

It is worth learning how the many protocols and services work, since they are so easy to install and configure in Linux.

SSH, RDP, and DNS can be installed and learned, among others.

Linux can even help you hone your proficiency using typed commands in the Terminal window. Here's where some of the real power of Linux comes into play. The ease of installing apps and configuring the OS will become apparent, after you learn the commands, such as `apt-get` and `sudo`.

You could, for example, install multiple apps or update all your installed apps, with a single command.

Running Linux from a USB flash drive

Instead of installing Linux on a computer, why not boot from a USB flash drive? What you'll actually be doing is running a temporary OS, which won't write data to the hard drive, and will *forget* whatever you did when you shut it down.

To run Ubuntu from a USB flash drive, you'll need to have a bootable live Linux USB drive, like the one you prepared for the previous chapter, to install Ubuntu on a PC.

After booting from the Linux USB drive, you'll reach the following screen:

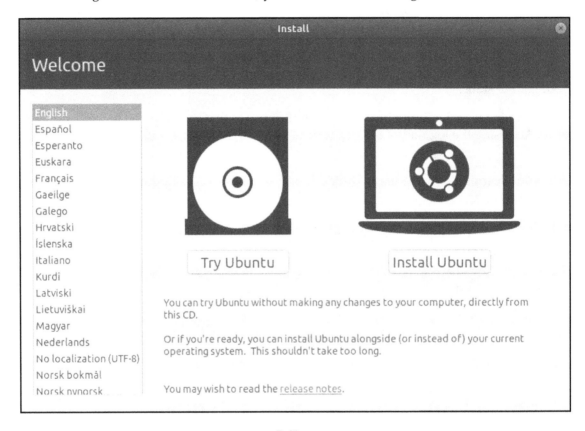

Try Ubuntu

Click **Try Ubuntu** and then Ubuntu will load without installing to the hard drive.

When you shut down the temporary OS, everything you did will be *forgotten*, providing additional security and privacy.

So, keep that in mind when deciding how to access the Dark Web. There are always multiple ways to do so, with varying levels of security. Choose what's best for you.

Summary

To sum up this chapter, Linux is a very flexible and customizable OS. With it comes a wide user base, which shares its knowledge, giving you accessible help, to perform almost anything you might want to do with it.

Play around with Linux, try out the many available distributions, and find one that is the best match for what you want to do with it. You will probably find that there is a lot of added value to it, other than using it as a simple desktop computer.

In the next chapter, we'll go over the process of installing and using the Tor browser on Linux.

Questions

1. What is Linux?
2. What is a distribution?
3. Who invented Linux?

    A. John Lin

    B. Linus Torvalds

    C. Linda Evans

Further reading

The following resources might be interesting if you'd like to delve deeper into the topics included this chapter:

- https://www.ubuntu.com/
- https://www.linux.org/
- https://www.linuxfoundation.org/

Accessing the Dark Web with Tor Browser

5

In the previous chapter, we installed Ubuntu Linux.

Now, we will discuss installing Tor Browser on Linux, in a few different ways, using a *standard* Linux distribution. When I say *standard*, I mean a distribution that is in common desktop use, and not a security-focused one, like the ones we will discuss in the following chapters. We'll learn how to install Tor Browser, and how to use it.

We will learn about the following topics in this chapter:

- What is Tor Browser?
- Installing Tor on Linux
- The Tor Project's recommendations on the safe use of Tor

What is Tor Browser?

According to the Tor Project website:

> *'Tor is free software and an open network that helps you defend against traffic analysis, a form of network surveillance that threatens personal freedom and privacy, confidential business activities and relationships, and state security.*
> *The Tor network is a group of volunteer-operated servers that allows people to improve their privacy and security on the Internet. Tor's users employ this network by connecting through a series of virtual tunnels rather than making a direct connection, thus allowing both organizations and individuals to share information over public networks without compromising their privacy. Along the same line, Tor is an effective censorship circumvention tool, allowing its users to reach otherwise blocked destinations or content. Tor can also be used as a building block for software developers to create new communication tools with built-in privacy features.'*

In other words, Tor (which is an acronym for **The Onion Router**, by the way) is a privacy focused network that hides your traffic, by routing it through multiple random servers on the Tor network.

So, instead of the packets that make up your communication with another party (person or organization), going from point A to B directly, using Tor, they will jump all over the place, between multiple servers, before reaching point B, hiding the trail.

Additionally, the packets that make up the traffic (or communication) in the Tor network are wrapped in special layers, which only show the previous server or step that the packet came from, and the next step, hiding the entire route effectively.

Tor Browser is a web browser, based on Firefox that was created for the purpose of accessing the Tor network, securely and privately.

Now, I'm going to say something that may surprise you.

Even if you use Tor, this doesn't mean that you're secure. Why is that? Because Tor Browser has software vulnerabilities, same as every other browser. It's also based on Firefox, so it inherits some of its vulnerabilities from there as well.

You can minimize attack vectors by applying common security sense, and by employing various tools to try to limit or prevent malicious activity, related to infecting Tor Browser or the host running it.

OK, let's move on to the juicy part: installing Tor on Linux.

Installing Tor on Linux

Installing software on Linux is usually very easy. There are several ways to install Tor Browser, and as I mentioned, we'll discuss a few in this chapter.

Let's start with a *classic* installation, by accessing the Tor Project website, via a browser. The default browser that ships with Ubuntu is Firefox, which is what we'll use.

Although you might think that this would be the best way to install Tor Browser, it's actually the least secure, since the Tor Project website is continuously targeted by hackers and might have any number of security or privacy issues on it.

Instead of just downloading Tor Browser and immediately installing it (which is dangerous), you can either download the file and verify its hash (to verify that it is indeed the correct one), or you could install it through other methods, for example, via the Terminal, by using Linux commands, or from the Ubuntu Software Center.

We'll start by going over the steps to download Tor Browser from the Tor Project website:

1. After booting your Linux installation, open your browser
2. Enter the following address and navigate to it: `https://www.torproject.org/download/download-easy.html.en#linux`.

Notice that the URL takes you directly to the Linux download section of the Tor Project website.

I usually prefer this direct method, rather than starting with Google (or any other search engine), searching for Tor, and then accessing the Tor Project website, since, as you may know, Google collects information about users accessing it, and the whole idea of this book is to maintain our privacy and security. Also, always verify that you're accessing the Tor Project website via HTTPS.

3. Choose the correct architecture (32 or 64 bit), and click the **Download** link.

4. You'll be able to choose what you want to do with the file—open it with Ubuntu's Archive Manager, or save it to a location on the disk:

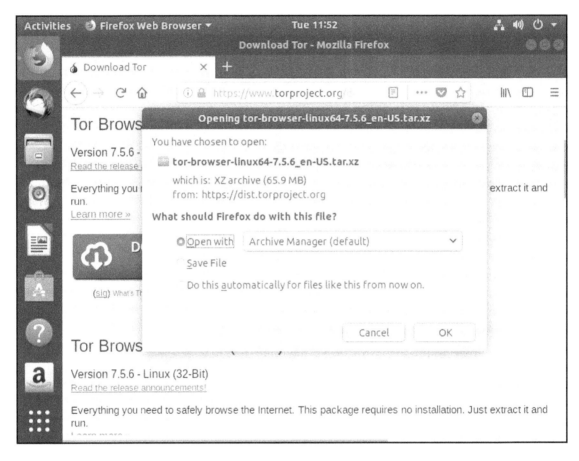

Downloading Tor Browser

Again, the quickest way to go would be to open the compressed file, but the more secure way would be to download the file and to verify its hash, before doing anything else.

The Tor Project provides **GNU Privacy Guard** (**GPG**) signature files, with each version of Tor Browser. You will need to install GnuPG on your Linux OS, if it isn't there already, in order to be able to verify the hash of the browser package.

To do so, just open the Terminal and type in the following:

```
sudo apt install gnupg
```

Enter your password when required, and the installation will commence.

Most Linux installations already include gnupg, as can be seen in the following screenshot:

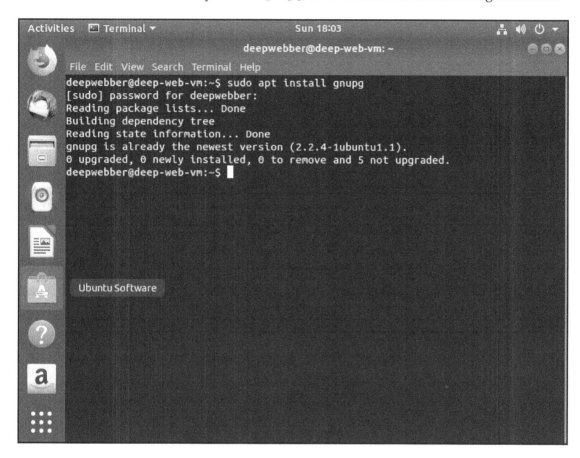

Installing GnuPG

After installing GnuPG, you need to import the key that signed the package. According to the Tor Project website, the Tor Browser import key is 0x4e2C6e8793298290.

The Tor Project updates and changes the keys from time to time, so you can always navigate to: https://www.torproject.org/docs/verifying-signatures.html.en to find the current import key, if the one in the book doesn't work.

The command to import the key is as follows:

```
gpg --keyserver pool.sks-keyservers.net --recv-keys 0x4e2C6e8793298290
```

This is followed by this:

```
gpg --fingerprint 0x4e2C6e8793298290
```

This will tell you whether the key fingerprint is correct.

You should see the following:

```
deepwebber@deep-web-vm:~$ gpg --fingerprint 0x4e2c6e8793298290
pub   rsa4096 2014-12-15 [C] [expires: 2020-08-24]
      EF6E 286D DA85 EA2A 4BA7  DE68 4E2C 6E87 9329 8290
uid           [ unknown] Tor Browser Developers (signing key) <torbrowser@torpr
oject.org>
sub   rsa4096 2016-08-24 [S] [expires: 2018-08-24]
sub   rsa4096 2018-05-26 [S] [expires: 2020-09-12]

deepwebber@deep-web-vm:~$ 
```

Verify key fingerprint

Now, you need to download the `.asc` file, which is found on the **Tor Browser Downloads** page, next to the relevant package of the browser (it appears as `sig`, short for signature):

Tor Browser Downloads			
		To start using Tor Browser, download the file for your preferred language. This file can be saved wherever is convenient, e.g. the Desktop or a USB flash drive.	
Stable Tor Browser			
Language	Microsoft Windows (7.5.6)	Apple MacOS (7.5.6)	GNU/Linux (7.5.6)
English (en-US)	32/64-bit *(sig)*	64-bit *(sig)*	32-bit *(sig)* • 64-bit *(sig)*
العربية (ar)	32/64-bit *(sig)*	64-bit *(sig)*	32-bit *(sig)* • 64-bit *(sig)*
Deutsch (de)	32/64-bit *(sig)*	64-bit *(sig)*	32-bit *(sig)* • 64-bit *(sig)*
Español (es-ES)	32/64-bit *(sig)*	64-bit *(sig)*	32-bit *(sig)* • 64-bit *(sig)*
فارسی (fa)	32/64-bit *(sig)*	64-bit *(sig)*	32-bit *(sig)* • 64-bit *(sig)*
Français (fr)	32/64-bit *(sig)*	64-bit *(sig)*	32-bit *(sig)* • 64-bit *(sig)*

ASC file location

You can find the Tor Browser download page here: `https://www.torproject.org/projects/torbrowser.html`

Now, you can verify the signature of the package, using the ASC file.

To do so, enter the following command in the Terminal:

```
gpg --verify tor-browser-linux64-7.5.6_en-US.tar.xz.asc tor-browser-
linux64-7.5.6_en-US.tar.xz
```

Note the `64` that I marked in bold. If your OS is 32-bit, change the number to `32`.

The result you should get is as follows:

```
deepwebber@deep-web-vm:~/Downloads$ gpg --verify tor-browser-linux64-7.5.6_en-U
S.tar.xz.asc tor-browser-linux64-7.5.6_en-US.tar.xz
gpg: Signature made Sat 23 Jun 2018 22:36:16 IDT
gpg:                using RSA key D1483FA6C3C07136
gpg: Good signature from "Tor Browser Developers (signing key) <torbrowser@torp
roject.org>" [unknown]
gpg: WARNING: This key is not certified with a trusted signature!
gpg:          There is no indication that the signature belongs to the owner.
Primary key fingerprint: EF6E 286D DA85 EA2A 4BA7  DE68 4E2C 6E87 9329 8290
     Subkey fingerprint: A430 0A6B C93C 0877 A445  1486 D148 3FA6 C3C0 7136
deepwebber@deep-web-vm:~/Downloads$
```

Verifying the signature

After verifying the hash (signature) of the Tor Browser package, you can install it.

You can do so by either:

- Double-clicking the Tor Browser package file (which will open up the Archive Manager program), clicking **Extract**, and choosing the location of your choice.
- Right-clicking the file and choosing **Extract here** or **Extract to** and choosing a location.

After extracting, perform the following steps:

1. Navigate to the location you defined.
2. Double-click on the `Start-tor-browser.desktop` file to launch Tor Browser.

3. Press **Trust and Launch** in the window that appears:

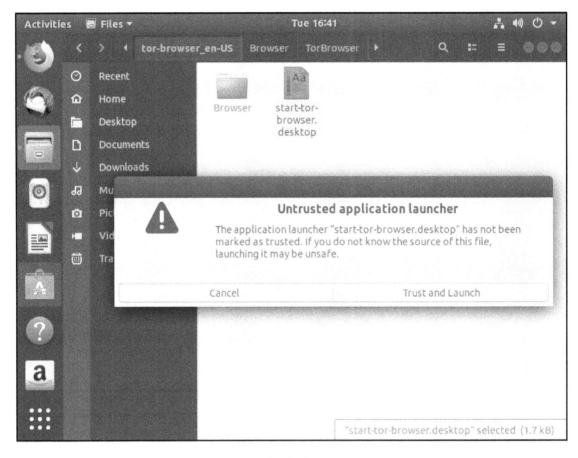

Launching Tor

Notice that the filename and icon changed to **Tor Browser**.

4. Press **Connect** and you will be connected to the Tor network, and will be able to browse it, using Tor Browser:

Connecting to Tor

Before we discuss using Tor Browser, let's talk about alternative ways to install it, for example, by using the Ubuntu Software application.

1. Start by clicking on the Ubuntu Software icon:

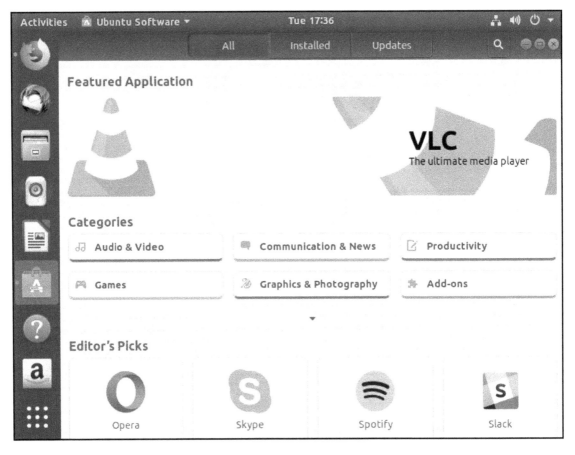

Ubuntu Software

2. Search for Tor Browser, then click on the relevant result:

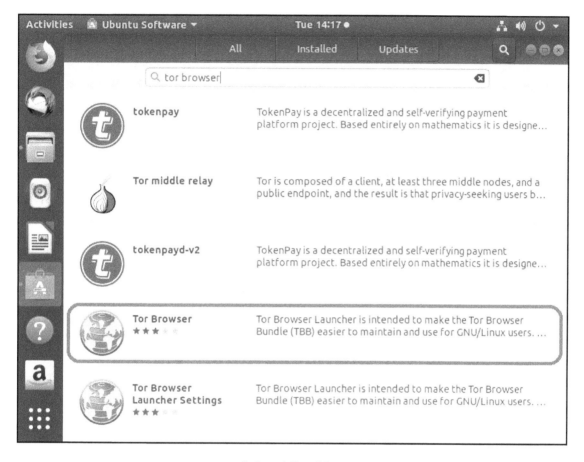

Tor Browser in Ubuntu Software

3. Then, click **Install**.
4. After entering your password, the installation process will start. When it ends, click **Launch** to start Tor Browser.

Installing Tor Browser via the Terminal, from the downloaded package

Another way to install Tor is to use commands, via the Terminal.

There are several ways to do so, as follows:

1. First, download the required Tor Browser package from the website
2. Verify the download, as we discussed before, and then keep the Terminal open
3. Navigate to the location where you downloaded Tor, by entering the following command:

   ```
   cd path/Tor_Browser_Directory
   ```

   For example, note the following:

   ```
   cd /downloads/tor-browser_en_US
   ```

4. Then, launch Tor Browser by running the following:

   ```
   ./start-tor-browser.desktop
   ```

 Never launch Tor as root (or with the sudo command).

Installing the Tor Browser entirely via the Terminal

Next, we'll discuss how to install Tor entirely via the Terminal:

1. First, launch the Terminal, as before.
2. Then, execute the following command:

   ```
   sudo apt install torbrowser-launcher
   ```

   This command will install Tor Browser.

 We need root access to install an app, not to launch it.

3. You can then run Tor by executing the following command:

   ```
   ./start-tor-browser.desktop
   ```

Tor Project recommendations on the safe use of Tor

The following is taken from the Tor Project website (`https://www.torproject.org/projects/torbrowser.html.en`), and are their recommendations on how to stay safe while using Tor.

1. Use Tor Browser.
2. Don't torrent over Tor.
3. Don't enable or install browser plugins.
4. Use HTTPS versions of websites.
5. Don't open documents downloaded through Tor while online.
6. Use bridges and/or find company.
7. Tor attempts to prevent attackers from learning what websites you browse to. But, it doesn't prevent anybody watching your traffic from detecting that you're using Tor. You can reduce this risk by using a Tor bridge relay, (`https://www.torproject.org/docs/bridges.html.en`), rather than connecting directly to the public Tor network.

But, before firing up Tor Browser, let's remember a few important things about accessing the Dark Web, or even surfing the internet, using Tor Browser. Your ISP (and thus your government or the NSA) will be able to detect you're using Tor Browser. This can draw the attention of the powers that be to yourself, and naturally, we don't want that. So, to prevent this, we need to use a **Virtual Private Network** (**VPN**). To use a VPN, you need to install a VPN client on your computer.

A VPN provides additional privacy and security, while Tor Browser provides anonymity. Combined, you are as protected as you can be without extreme measures.

The question arises—which VPN should I use?

Well, there are several basic guidelines you should follow when choosing a VPN:

- First, the encryption level. 128-bit is OK, but 256-bit encryption is much better (much harder to crack).
- Also, choose a VPN that doesn't save logs, either locally or on the VPN provider's servers.

- One of the issues that many VPNs face is unexpected disconnections, which can expose your IP address to the ISP, or the world, so remember to choose one that has a kill switch (if you remember, I explained about this in `Chapter 4`, *Installing a Linux Virtual Machine*; it's a mechanism that disconnects the computer's internet connection, if the VPN disconnects unexpectedly).
- Choose a VPN that is designed to prevent IP and DNS leaks (operating system and browser vulnerabilities can leak, or expose, your DNS requests and IP address, if not prevented).
- Choose a VPN that provides IP addresses from other countries (and choose a country different than your own when configuring it).

There are many free and paid VPNs out there. Their installation may vary, but each will provide own instructions. Just be sure to obtain one that has the capabilities I've mentioned.

Okay, now that we've seen how we can install Tor Browser and understand that we need a VPN (and have hopefully chosen one), let's start using Tor Browser.

Start Tor Browser, using any of the options listed previously. After you reach Tor Browser's home page, you can navigate to sites on the Dark Web. These sites are in the `.onion` domain (for example, `https://darkwebsite.onion`).

You can also surf *regular* internet sites, but, they will function sluggishly, due to the routing that the Tor network performs, and the fact that cookies, scripts, add-ons, and other extensions that usually work in our regular browsers don't work in Tor Browser.

But, if used correctly (VPN + taking precautions), you can stay anonymous on the internet (and the Dark Web, of course).

Remember that Tor Browser is a web browser, like Chrome, Firefox, Edge, Internet Explorer, but much more private and anonymous, so you can perform all the same basic actions.

Here is a list of a few `.onion` sites you can start with:

- `https://www.facebookcorewwwi.onion/`

    Yes, it's Facebook.

    Facebook provides this for use in countries that censor using it (not really for anonymity):

- `http://3g2upl4pq6kufc4m.onion/`

An excellent, private, alternative to Google. Search behavior and activity isn't logged, so the search experience is a little different (more like a pre-Google era search experience):

- `https://www.propub3r6espa33w.onion/`

The first online publication that won a Pulitzer prize also has a `.onion` domain. There, you can find many articles and information, published both anonymously and publicly, about many, many topics.

Here, you can see a screenshot of the Propublica site, as accessed via Tor Browser:

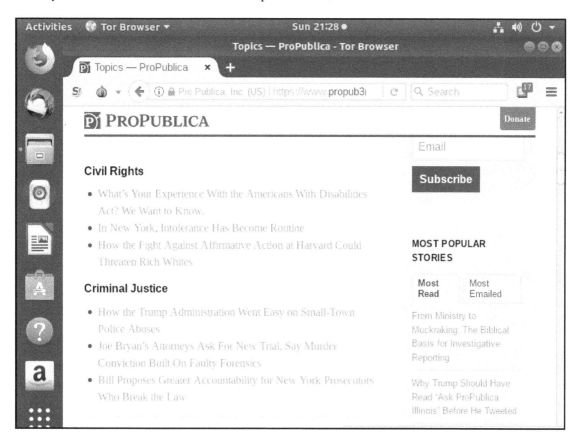

Propublica

The Hidden Wiki: think of this as Wikipedia with all stops removed. A lot of information is available at `http://zqktlwi4fecvo6ri.onion/wiki/index.php/Main_Page`

There are also Dark Web search engines, such as the following:

- **Tor Onionland**: Search engine with close to 60,000 `.onion` websites and almost 5 million indexed pages. (`http://onionlandbakyt3j.onion/`)
- **Torch**: Search engine with almost 500,000 indexed `.onion` services. (`http://xmh57jrzrnw6insl.onion/`)
- **Not Evil**: Search engine with over 32 million `.onion` indexed links. (`http://hss3uro2hsxfogfq.onion/`)
- **Candle**: A basic search engine that completely ignores operators, parentheses, and quotes; just words. (`http://gjobqjj7wyczbqie.onion.link/`)
- **Grams**: Market search engine only for finding labor, digital, and physical items you can purchase with Bitcoin and other currencies. (`http://grams7enqfy4nieo.onion/`)
- **Haystak**: Searches `.onion` services and claims to have more than 1.5 billion pages from almost 300,000 websites (many are already obsolete). (`http://haystakvxad7wbk5.onion/`)

Many of the sites listed may not work when you try them. This happens since their addresses change frequently. But, I listed them to help you get on your way, browsing the Deep Web. The best way to learn how to access the Dark Web is simply by doing so.

So, what are you waiting for?

Summary

In this chapter, we talked about Tor, Tor Browser, how to install it in several ways, and how to use it.

In the next few chapters, we'll talk about several privacy- and security-focused operating systems that can be used to access the Dark Web in a safe (relatively, anyway) manner.

Questions

1. List at least four recommendations for safe use of Tor Browser.

    A. Use Tor Browser.

    B. Don't torrent over Tor.

    C. Don't enable or install browser plugins.

    D. Use HTTPS versions of websites.

    E. Don't open documents downloaded through Tor while online.

    F. Use bridges and/or find company.

2. Tor Browser is based on which of the following browsers?

    A. Chrome

    B. Internet Explorer

    C. Edge

    D. Firefox

    E. Opera

    F. Safari

3. What is the Terminal command to start Tor Browser?

Further reading

The following resource might be interesting if you'd like to delve deeper into the topics included in this chapter:

- https://www.torproject.org/projects/torbrowser.html.en

Installing Tails OS 6

Online privacy and security are critical. Sadly, many individuals, or groups, have less-than-honorable intentions when using the internet, the Dark Web, or any other online medium. We need to take steps to protect ourselves, and, as we've discussed previously, there are many ways to do so. One of them is by using privacy and security-oriented OSes. One of them is Tails.

In the previous chapter, we learned about Tor and how to install and use it.

In this chapter, we will learn the following topics:

- What is Tails OS?
- Tails OS installation prerequisites
- Downloading Tails OS
- Installing Tails OS

What is Tails OS?

Tails, which is short for **The Amnesic Incognito Live System**, is a Debian Linux-based, security- and privacy-focused OS, intended to be run from a USB flash drive or a DVD. As such, Tails doesn't leave any traces on the original OS installed on the PC, either in the memory or the filesystem. This, of course, helps with privacy. The Tor Project funds the development of Tails, along with Mozilla, the Freedom of the Press Foundation, and the Debian Project.

As an OS, Tails ships with several default applications, focused on security. For example, Tails uses Tor by default to connect to the internet. Its default browser is Tor Browser. All outgoing communication is routed through the Tor network, and non-anonymous connections are not allowed. It includes applications to encrypt data, a password generator, and tools to minimize the risk when connecting to the internet (all communication, including emails and instant messaging, are encrypted by default).

All in all, it's one of the most secure OSes out there.

Some of the security features supplied by Tails, by default (Tor Browser is the default browser in Tails OS), are as follows:

- **AppArmor confinement**: Enforces specific sets of rules on applications, limiting their access in the system.
- **HTTPS Encryption**: All traffic is encrypted by default.
- **HTTPS Everywhere**: Thanks to a browser extension developed by the Electronic Frontier Foundation, for Firefox, Chrome, and Opera, communication with many major websites is encrypted, providing a more secure browsing experience.
- **Torbutton**: An extension developed for Tor Browser, to enhance security and privacy, which has multiple capabilities:
    - **Protection against dangerous JavaScript**: Limits and prevents dangerous JavaScript from running.
    - **Security slider**: Feature to manage Tor Browser security setting levels.
    - **New Identity feature**: This is intended to remove session information (cache, cookies, history, and so on), closes all web connections, erases the content of the clipboard, and closes all open tabs. (Having said that, to completely remove data, restart Tails.)
    - **NoScript**: Allows complete disabling of JavaScript.

But, even with all its security, privacy, and anonymity options, Tails has weaknesses.

For example (according to the Tails website documentation), note the following:

- Tails does not protect against compromised hardware—meaning that if an attacker gains physical access to the computer you are running Tails from, it can be unsafe.
- Tails can be compromised if installed on or plugged into untrusted systems—remember that you install or run Tails from a computer with its own OS. If that computer is compromised, this can lead to disruption of Tails' protective capabilities.
- Tails does not protect against BIOS or firmware attacks—attacks that target the computer's BIOS or firmware aren't protected by Tails.
- Tor exit nodes can eavesdrop on communications—the exit node, the last node in the Tor relay network, which connects to the destination server, is not encrypted, and this allows attackers to eavesdrop and capture the communication at that point. To protect yourself, it's recommended to use end-to-end encryption.

- Tails makes it clear that you are using Tor and probably Tails—even though you're using Tails and Tor for connecting, which will make it harder to identify you, your ISP, local network admin, or destination server, can identify that you are using Tor.

- Man-in-the-middle attacks—as I mentioned previously, the traffic between the exit node and the destination server is unencrypted, which allows attackers to perform a man-in-the-middle attack, where the attacker eavesdrops on the communication.

- Confirmation attacks (also known as end-to-end correlation)—traffic entering or exiting the Tor network can be measured and analyzed, which can lead to identifying you.

- Tails doesn't encrypt your documents by default—but, Tails ships with encryption tools, just for this purpose.

- Tails doesn't clear the metadata of your documents for you and doesn't encrypt the subject and other headers of your encrypted email messages—but, Tails provides tools to anonymize your documents.

- Tor doesn't protect you from a global adversary—a global adversary has the capability to monitor all traffic in a network simultaneously. Thus, they could potentially be able to perform statistical analysis on the traffic, to identify Tor circuits and then match the communication to destination servers.

- Tails doesn't magically separate your different contextual identities—performing multiple actions in the same session is inadvisable, as Tor has a tendency to reuse the same circuits in a given session. Restarting Tails will make sure that you prevent this.

- Tails doesn't make your passwords stronger—don't use weak passwords; need I say more?

- Tails is a work in progress—as with all software in development, bugs or security flaws can occur.

Bearing all of this in mind, we can minimize our risk by following best practices and common sense.

Tails OS installation prerequisites

As with all installations of software (OSes are software), we need to verify the installation requirements before beginning.

For Tails, the hardware installation requirements are as follows:

- A 64-bit x86-64 compatible processor (except for PowerPC or ARM)
- 2 GB of RAM
- A way to boot either from a DVD or USB flash drive

There are several ways to install and use Tails, depending on the OS of the computer on which you'll be installing Tails.

The time it takes and the complexity of the installation process is also affected by the *source computer*.

Tails can be installed from Windows, Debian, Ubuntu, or Mint Linux, or almost any other Linux distros. (macOS isn't really supported, but you can always install Tails as a virtual machine in macOS.)

Although I won't go into detail for all of the possible source OSes in this book, I will outline the general processes for most of them, and provide detailed instructions for Linux (Ubuntu).

Downloading Tails OS

Let's get started by downloading Tails OS in the following OSes.

Downloading Tails OS in Windows

1. Download the Tails OS ISO file from the Tails website: `https://tails.boum.org/install/win/index.en.html`.

2. It's highly recommended to verify the downloaded file's signature.

Downloading Tails OS in Linux

1. Navigate to the Tails OS download page:
   `https://tails.boum.org/install/download/index.en.html#install-inc-steps-download.inline.basic-openpgp`.
2. Download the Tails OS ISO file, either directly or via a Torrent client (I personally prefer the direct download option, as torrents can be insecure).

3. For security purposes, it's a good practice to verify the ISO file. The process is similar to what I talked about previously in the book. You need to download the Tails signature, and signing key, while, or after, you download the Tails OS ISO file.

4. You can download the signing key from here: `https://tails.boum.org/tails-signing.key`.

5. And, the signature file is available here: `https://tails.boum.org/torrents/files/tails-amd64-3.8.iso.sig`.

6. Save them in the same folder where you saved the ISO file.

7. To verify the downloaded file, using OpenPGP, run the following command in the Linux Terminal:

```
gpg --no-options --keyid-format 0xlong --verify tails-
amd64-3.8.iso.sig tails-amd64-3.8.iso
```

The result should be as follows:

```
gpg: Signature made Mon 25 Jun 2018 11:14:47 AM UTC
gpg: using EDDSA key CD4D4351AFA6933F574A9AFB90B2B4BD7AED235F
gpg: Good signature from "Tails developers <tails@boum.org>" [full]
gpg: aka "Tails developers (offline long-term identity key)
<tails@boum.org>" [full]
```

8. Always verify that there is no more than five days between the signature and the latest version of the ISO file.

Installing Tails OS

Let's move on to installing Tails OS in the following OSes.

Installing Tails OS in Windows

Installing Tails directly from Windows is not currently possible, but it can be done by using two USB sticks, and installing Tails on one, and then the other, as shown in the following steps:

1. Install Tails on one of the USB sticks, the *intermediary* one, using the Universal USB Installer (I mentioned it in `Chapter 4`, *Installing a Linux Virtual Machine*).

2. In the Universal USB Installer application interface, choose to install from the Tails OS ISO file you downloaded.

3. After installing Tails OS on the first USB stick, restart your computer and boot from the USB stick. You should boot into Tails, after a few seconds.

4. Now, plug in the second USB stick, go to **Applications | Tails | Tails Installer** (in Tails OS), and install Tails on it.

5. After the installation process ends, remove the first USB stick, restart the computer, and boot from the second USB stick.

You'll boot into Tails OS.

Installing Tails OS in Red Hat, Fedora (any Linux distro that isn't Debian, Ubuntu, or Mint) for browsing the Dark Web

The process here is basically the same as with Windows (install on the first USB stick, then on the second, then run from second).

The installation of the first USB stick is done using GNOME Disks (also known as **Disks**), and then, after rebooting from it, you'll use the Tails Installer to install Tails OS on the second USB stick.

The rest of this chapter will detail how to install Tails OS via Debian, Ubuntu, or Mint Linux distros.

Note that the software installation requirements are as follows:

- Debian 9 and higher
- Ubuntu 16.04 and higher
- Linux Mint 18 and higher

We will start by installing Tails Installer, which, in turn, will install Tails.

To do so, perform the following actions:

1. Start software and updates in Linux.
2. Verify that the **Community-maintained free and open-source software (universe)** option is selected:

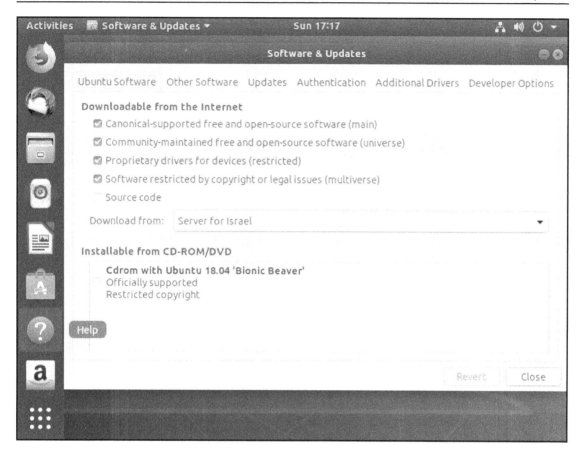

Community-maintained free and open-source software

3. Press the **Other Software** tab, and click on the **Add...** button.

4. In the APT line field, enter the following:

```
ppa:tails-team/tails-installer
```

5. And then, press the **Add Source** button. You will see the **Authentication Required** window, so enter your password and press **Authenticate**. Then, press **Close**.

6. Then, press **Reload** and wait for the package download process to finish.

7. Open the Terminal and run the following command to install the **Tails Installer** package:

```
sudo apt install tails-installer
```

Installing Tails from the command line

You can also download and install Tails from the command line, as shown in the following steps:

1. First, download the ISO image by running the following command in the Terminal:

```
wget --continue
http://dl.amnesia.boum.org/tails/stable/tails-amd64-3.9/tails-amd64
-3.9.iso
```

 Don't forget to verify the ISO file.

2. Next, install Tails Installer. Depending on your Linux distro (Debian, Ubuntu, or Mint), you'll need to run different commands in the next step, to add the required repositories.

Since we've been using Ubuntu, I'll start with the commands for it (they're the same for Mint).

There are two repositories to install—Tails PPA and universe.

 A **Personal Package Archive** (**PPA**) is custom software (or custom updates), not provided in Ubuntu, by default.
The Ubuntu version release cycle is every six months, so if you want to update applications between versions, or install new ones, which don't exist in the Ubuntu Software Center, you'll probably install a PPA.

Run the following commands to add them:

```
sudo add-apt-repository universe
sudo add-apt-repository ppa:tails-team/tails-installer
```

Debian needs the `backports` repository. To add it, run the following:

```
BACKPORTS='deb http://http.debian.net/debian/ stretch-backports main'
echo $BACKPORTS | sudo tee /etc/apt/sources.list.d/stretch-backports.list
&& echo "OK"
```

Then, in any of these distros, run the following command to update your lists of packages:

```
sudo apt update
```

The next step will be to prepare and install Tails on the USB flash drive:

1. Connect the USB flash drive to the computer, and then start the Tails Installer from Linux.
2. You can run the following command from Terminal:

```
sudo apt install tails-installer
```

Or, you can go to Ubuntu Software and search for Tails.

3. Press the Tails Installer icon:

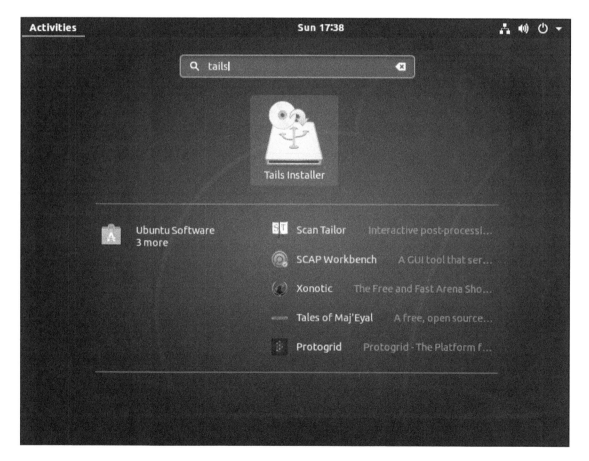

Tails Installer startup

4. When Tails Installer loads, press the folder icon next to the button that displays **None**, and locate the ISO file you downloaded previously.

5. Under **Target USB stick**, choose the USB flash drive you connected to the computer, as follows:

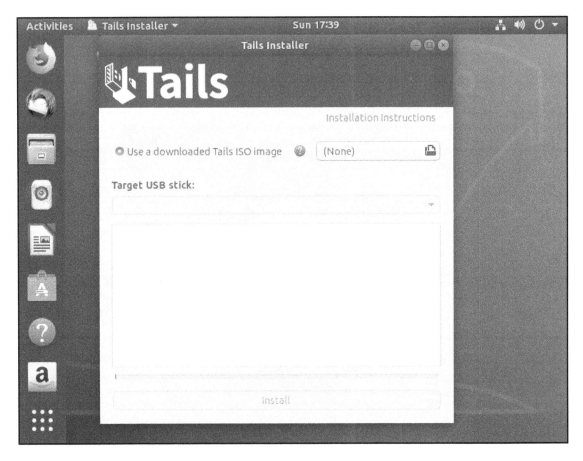

Tails Installer

6. Press **Install**, go over the displayed warning, and click **Yes** to confirm.

7. You will be asked to enter your password twice during the installation process, after which you will see an **Installation Complete** message, which you can close.

That's it. You can now boot your computer from the USB flash drive, and start Tails.

After booting from the Tails USB flash drive, you'll reach the Boot Loader Menu:

Tails Boot Loader Menu

You can press the *Enter* key or wait until the startup process continues.

After another 30-60 seconds, the Tails Greeter screen will appear, where you can choose your language, keyboard layout, and format.

Now, press **Start Tails**:

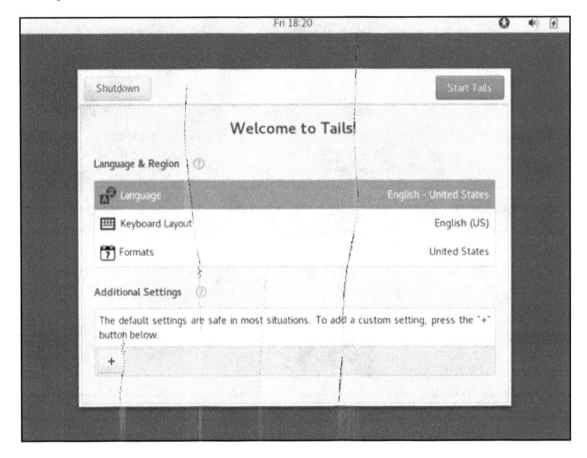

Tails greeter

After Tails starts, you'll reach the Tails desktop, from which you'll be able to connect to a network by going to the system menu, in the upper-right part of the screen (click the little drop-down arrow):

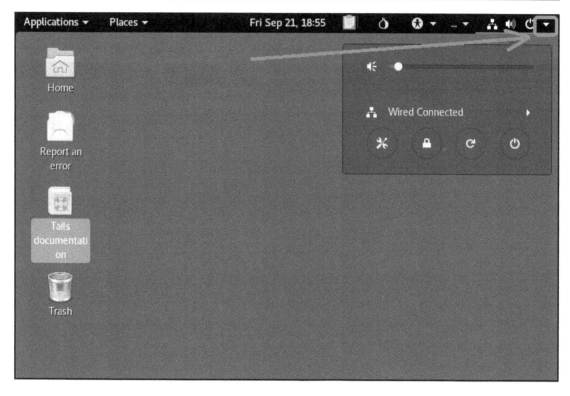

Tails System Menu

Wired connections are configured automatically; for Wi-Fi, press **Wi-Fi** (it can also display **Wi-Fi Not Connected**) and then select **Network**. Choose the required network and connect.

Now, you can run Tor Browser and surf the Deep and Surface Web much more anonymously and privately.

Using Tor Browser in Tails is similar to Linux, using the graphical user interface, rather than Terminal, as shown here:

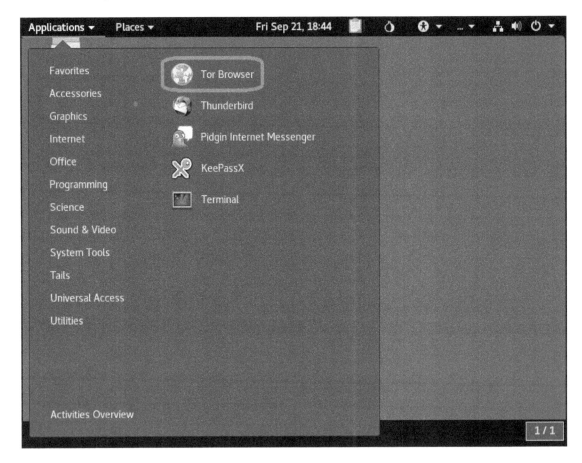

Tor Browser in Tails

Go to the **Applications** menu, and press the Tor Browser icon.

You're done. You can now start using Tor Browser on Tails OS, to access the Dark Web.

Summary

This chapter was more hands-on and focused than previous chapters.

As we go along, I expect that your comfort with technical actions will grow, if you weren't technically proficient before reading this book, so it will get easier. But if it doesn't, you'll have the step-by-step instructions in this book.

Tails is a very privacy-focused OS that may take getting used to. If actions take more time, or work in a different manner, always remember that there's a trade-off between security/privacy and speed or comfort/ease of use.

In the next chapter, we'll continue with installations of additional OSes. After trying them out, choose the one that best fits your requirements.

Questions

1. What are the Linux software installation requirements for Tails OS?
2. What Terminal command starts the Tails Installer application?
3. What are the Tails OS hardware installation requirements?

Further reading

The following resource might be interesting if you'd like to go deeper into the subjects of this chapter:

- https://tails.boum.org/

Installing Whonix 7

In the last chapter, we focused on installing Tails and accessing the Deep Web with it. Whonix is designed for advanced security and privacy. It's a heavily reconfigured Linux Debian that runs inside multiple virtual machines, providing a substantial layer of protection from malware and IP address leaks.

Whonix is the only operating system designed to be run inside a VM and paired with Tor.

In this chapter, we'll learn how to install and use Whonix to browse the Deep Web.

We will discuss the following topics:

- What Whonix is
- Whonix installation and pre-requisites
- Using Tor Browser with Whonix

What is Whonix?

Whonix is another OS focused on security and privacy. It's open source, and hence free to download and use. It's based on Linux (Debian) and Tor is implemented into it, to force all network connections through Tor (or be blocked). This is done automatically and is virtually system wide. Whonix is the only OS to work this way, so far.

Whonix was designed with the concept of VMs in mind. Desktop applications come pre-installed and are pre-configured with safety in mind. (It's also possible to install custom applications)

Whonix has two parts: the Whonix-Gateway VM and the Whonix-Workstation VM. The first runs Tor processes and acts as a gateway, while the second runs applications on an isolated network. There are several benefits to this design:

- All connections are routed through Tor
- Applications and servers can be run anonymously over the internet
- DNS leaks are not possible
- Malware with root privileges can't detect the user's real IP address
- User errors that could lead to threats are minimized

Most of the pre-installed applications, which connect to networks, use a dedicated Tor SocksPort. This helps with stream isolation and helps prevent identity correlation. Applications using Tor's DNS and/or Transport can be optionally disabled.

Whonix can be installed on hypervisors such VirtualBox, KVM, and more interestingly, on Qubes OS, to enhance security and anonymity. According to the Whonix website, it can help to do the following:

- Disguise a user's IP address
- Prevent ISP spying
- Prevent websites from identifying the user
- Prevent malware from identifying the user
- Circumvent censorship

Whonix can do this by providing the following features (among others):

- Anonymous browsing, by using Tor Browser for internet browsing
- Anonymous instant messaging, using apps such as Tox and Ricochet, routed through Tor
- Anonymous file sharing with OnionShare (`https://www.whonix.org/wiki/Onionshare`)
- Hiding Host location (`https://www.whonix.org/wiki/Hosting_Location_Hidden_Services`)
- Sending anonymous emails without registration
- Anonymous Java/JavaScript
- Full IP/DNS protocol leak protection
- Hiding Tor and Whonix use from network observers
- Hiding installed software from network observers
- Preventing anyone from learning the user's IP address

- Protecting user privacy
- Almost any application is torified
- Can torify other operating systems (such as Qubes and Windows)
- Connecting to a proxy, VPN, or SSH before Tor or vice versa
- Tunneling to other networks through Tor, such as GNUnet, I2P, and more
- PGP-encrypted email with Mozilla Thunderbird, Enigmail, and TorBirdy

Whonix installation and prerequisites

The following are the supported platforms:

- Qubes
- KVM
- VirtualBox
- PC x86 compatible

The minimum hardware resource requirement is as follows:

- 1 GB free RAM
- 10 GB free hard drive space

The minimum (Qubes 4.X) requirements are as follows:

- A 64-bit Intel or AMD processor
- 4 GB RAM
- 32 GB disk space
- Legacy boot mode—required for R3.0 and earlier; UEFI is supported beginning with R3.1
- Intel VT-x with EPT (`https://en.wikipedia.org/wiki/Second_Level_Address_Translation#Extended_Page_Tables`) or AMD-V with RVI (`https://en.wikipedia.org/wiki/Second_Level_Address_Translation#Rapid_Virtualization_Indexing`)
- Intel VT-d or AMD-Vi (also known as AMD IOMMU)—required for effective isolation of network VMs

Whonix download

Whonix can be downloaded ready for the various supported hypervisors (Windows, Linux, OS X, and Qubes), from the following URL:

```
https://www.whonix.org/wiki/Download
```

Whonix installation

For this hands on installation, we'll use VirtualBox. You can find VirtualBox for download at the following URL:

```
https://www.virtualbox.org/wiki/Downloads
```

Perform the following steps to install Whonix:

1. Download the version that's appropriate for your host operating system and install it
2. Install VirtualBox in the manner that's appropriate for your host OS
3. Import the Whonix-Gateway and Whonix-Workstation OVA files into VirtualBox, as an appliance
4. Double-click on the Whonix-Gateway and Whonix-Workstation objects in VirtualBox to start them
5. Finish the configuration
6. Start Tor Browser

You can see the step-by-step instructions (for steps 3-6) here: `https://www.whonix.org/wiki/VirtualBox/CLI`

To import Whonix into VirtualBox, see the following:

1. In VirtualBox, Click **File | Import Appliance**:

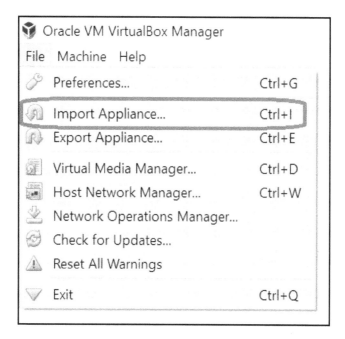

Import the virtual appliance

2. Click the Choose icon (it looks like a folder) and select the `Whonix-Gateway.ova` file, which you downloaded previously and then click **Open**:

Appliance to import

3. Click **Next** and then **Import** without changing any settings:

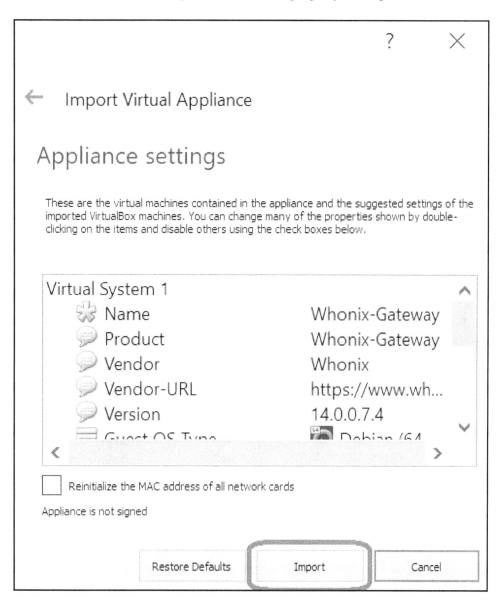

Appliance settings

4. Click **Agree** when the **Software License Agreement** window appears:

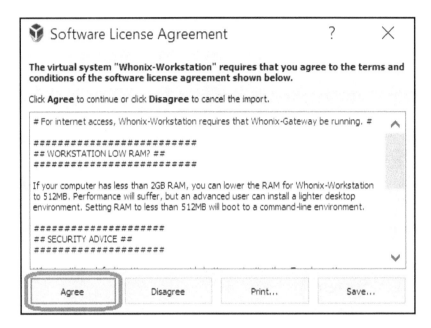

Whonix Software License Agreement

- Wait for the progress bar to complete the import
- Repeat these steps for the `Whonix-Workstation.ova` file
- Now, start the Whonix-Gateway followed by Whonix-Workstation:

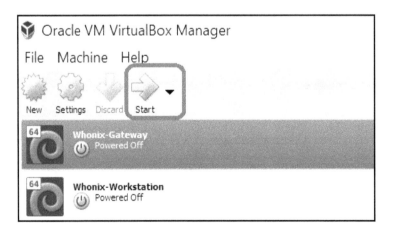

Start Whonix VMs

If you need to log on, these are the default credentials:

- **Username**: user
- **Password**: changeme

5. Configure network connectivity in Whonix-Gateway:

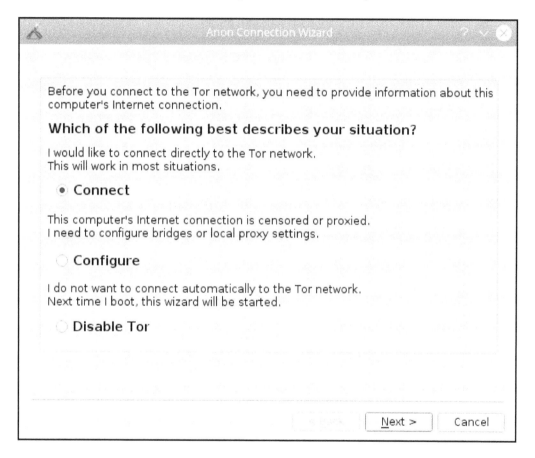

Anon Connection Wizard

6. After the **Anon Connection Wizard** finishes, you'll continue the setup process, until Tor is fully configured:

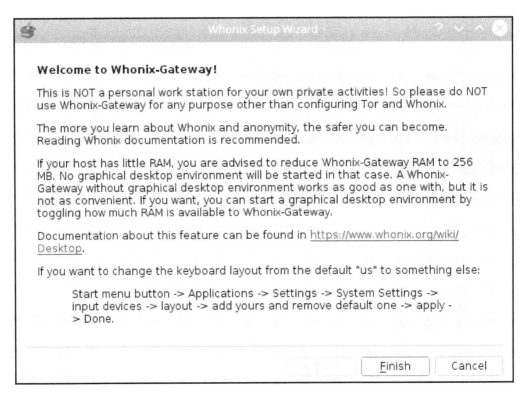

Finish Whonix installation

It's highly recommended to change passwords on both Whonix-Gateway and Whonix-Workstation for both the user and root accounts. (Qubes-Whonix users can skip this section.)

To do so,

1. Open Console, the Whonix terminal, by going to the following: **Start menu** | **Applications** | **System** | **Terminal**.

2. Log in as `root` by running the following:

```
sudo su
```

3. Then, run the following:

passwd

4. And then run the following command:

passwd user

Let's look at the following output:

```
user@host:~$ sudo su

We trust you have received the usual lecture from the local System
Administrator. It usually boils down to these three things:

    #1) Respect the privacy of others.
    #2) Think before you type.
    #3) With great power comes great responsibility.

[sudo] password for user:
root@host:/home/user#
root@host:/home/user#
root@host:/home/user# passwd
Enter new UNIX password:
Retype new UNIX password:
passwd: password updated successfully
root@host:/home/user# passwd user
Enter new UNIX password:
Retype new UNIX password:
passwd: password updated successfully
root@host:/home/user#
```

Change passwords

Using Tor Browser with Whonix

To start browsing the Dark Web, you can start Tor Browser, by going to **Start Menu** | **Favorites** | **Privacy Browser**, as can be seen in the following:

Start Tor Browser in Whonix

Then, you'll see the Whonix Tor Browser window:

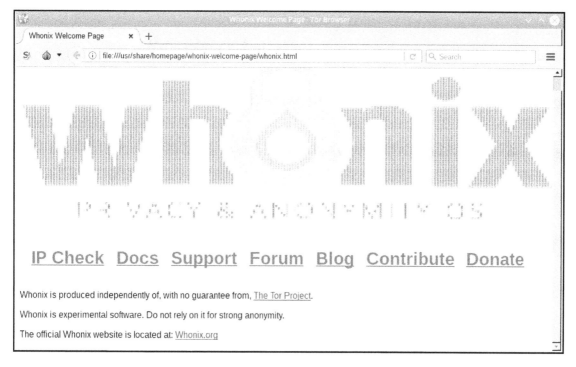

Whonix Tor Browser

Browsing is done as usual, by entering the URL of `.onion` sites.

Summary

In this chapter, we talked about Whonix, how to install it, and its basic use. We discussed what makes Whonix unique, and how it helps protect the user's privacy and security. We saw how easy it is to access the Dark Web using Whonix since it was developed for that purpose. There's no need to install or configure anything after installing the OS.

As we've discussed, Whonix works with two VMs, one acting as the gateway and securing the traffic, and the other as the workstation, providing a desktop interface for the user. Always remember to start Whonix-Gateway first, to verify that the traffic is going through it, and then turn on the Whonix-Workstation.

Questions

1. What makes Whonix unique?
2. What other operating systems are designed to work with Whonix?

Further reading

The following resource might be of interest if you'd like to go deeper into the issues discussed in this chapter:

- `https://www.whonix.org/wiki/Main_Page`

Installing Qubes OS

8

Qubes OS, a Xen-based operating system, which is also considered extremely secure, will be the focus of this chapter.

Qubes OS operates under the assumption that it has already been breached, so every application is run in its own virtual environment.

In this chapter, we will learn how to install and use Qubes OS for accessing the Deep Web

- What is Qubes OS?
- How to install Qubes OS
- Accessing the Dark Web with Qubes

What is Qubes OS?

Qubes OS is another security, privacy, and anonymity-focused operating system. The developers designed it with the belief that, currently, there's no tool or software that can completely protect us from **zero-day attacks** (attacks that exploit software vulnerabilities, which have, so far, not been discovered by the software vendor, and hence they have no patches or fixes yet, and can be exploited by hackers) and sophisticated hackers, who use tools and attacks that can bypass most, if not all, of an organization's defenses, be it firewall, antivirus, or another tool.

So, they came up with a great idea: compartmentalization, separating what we do on the computer into securely isolated compartments, which the developers named **qubes**.

Applications' hardware and sessions can be separated into their own secure qube, providing strict separation from the other qubes, and, this way, if the user surfs to a compromised website, and the user's browser is infected by malware, no other part of the user's computer or applications will be affected (effectively preventing the attacker from reaching anything *of worth* and allowing the user to deal with the issue).

The same idea works with running an infected application.

Even though almost everything in Qubes OS is isolated, the user experience provides a unified interface, with different colors for window borders, differentiating the various applications and locations, which allows for quick identification of the security level that the user gave the app, location, and so on.

Hardware is also isolated, so the common targets, such as USB controllers, network cards, and firewalls, are also protected.

Qubes also utilizes an interesting *Template* system, which provides locations to install software and to share resources, in a manner that's similar to virtual machines. These TemplateVMs are based on several OSes, such as Fedora (which is the default template), Ubuntu, Whonix, and Archlinux.

Not every app runs in its own qube. Each qube represents what the developers call a **security domain**. By default, all qubes are based on a single, common TemplateVM, (more TemplateVMs can be created if required). Qubes have read-only access to the filesystem of the template on which it's based. If a qube is ever compromised, the TemplateVM on which it's based (including any other qubes based on that specific TemplateVM) remain safe.

Installing Qubes with the default options will provide several default qubes: work, personal, and untrusted. Each qube is also assigned a **label**, which is one of several pre-defined colors. These labels are used to visually differentiate between qubes, and how you interpret them, or use them, is up to you, the user.

In previous chapters, we talked about live CD OSes (OSes that boot from USB or CDs and aren't installed on the computers hardware). They have many security advantages, but, according to Qubes OS developers, live CD OSes are still vulnerable. If these OSes get infected, everything in the OS is at risk, while with Qubes OS, only the specific qube would be infected and the rest of the OS stays safe.

Qubes installs with Xen, a bare-metal hypervisor, by default and is not intended to be installed as a virtual machine (or on a different hypervisor)

Preparing to install Qubes OS

First, download the ISO file from `https://www.qubes-os.org/downloads/`.

Remember, as always, to verify the signature of the downloaded file. There are several ways to get the Qubes Master Signing Key, which allows for the signature verification:

- Fetch it with GPG:

  ```
  $ gpg --fetch-keys
  https://keys.qubes-os.org/keys/qubes-master-signing-key.asc
  ```

- Download it from `https://keys.qubes-os.org/keys/qubes-master-signing-key.asc`, and then import it with GPG:

  ```
  $ gpg --import ./qubes-master-signing-key.asc
  ```

- Get it from a public `keyserver` (specified on first use with `--keyserver <URI>`, then saved in `~/.gnupg/gpg.conf`), as in the following example:

  ```
  $ gpg --keyserver pool.sks-keyservers.net --recv-keys
  0x427F11FD0FAA4B080123F01CDDFA1A3E36879494
  ```

- Next, obtain the Release Signing Key from the **Downloads** page on the Qubes website, or by fetching it with GPG:

  ```
  $ gpg --fetch-keys
  https://keys.qubes-os.org/keys/qubes-release-X-signing-key.asc
  ```

  If you downloaded the file, you will need to import it with GPG, as seen in the following command:

  ```
  $ gpg --import ./qubes-release-X-signing-key.asc
  ```

- Fianlly, verify the Qubes OS ISO file by running the following:

  ```
  $ gpg -v --verify Qubes-R4.0-x86_64.iso.asc Qubes-R4.0-x86_64.iso
  ```

If part of the message you see contains the following, then you're good to go: **Good signature from "Qubes OS Release X Signing Key"**.

Next, you need to transfer the ISO file to the DVD or USB flash drive. If you prefer to use a USB drive, then you just need to copy the ISO on to the USB device, for example, using `dd`:

```
dd if=FILENAME of= target device bs=1048576 && sync
```

According to the Qubes OS website:

> *"On Windows, you can use the Rufus tool. Be sure to select "DD image" mode (you need to do that **after** selecting the Qubes ISO):*
> ***Warning:*** *If you do that on Windows 10, you can only install Qubes without MediaTest, which isn't recommended."*

You can obtain Rufus from here: `https://rufus.akeo.ie/`.

 Universal USB Installer can also be used.

You can also install Qubes on a USB flash drive, as a Live CD/USB, with one specification: leave the option checked to **Automatically configure my Qubes installation to the disk(s) I selected and return me to the main menu**.

Hardware requirements

The minimum installation requirements are as follows:

- 64-bit Intel or AMD processor (AMD64)
- Intel VT-x with EPT or AMD-V with RVI
- Intel VT-d or AMD-Vi (in other words, AMD IOMMU)
- 4 GB RAM
- 32 GB disk space

The following are the recommended requirements:

- Fast SSD (strongly recommended)
- Intel IGP (strongly preferred):
    - Nvidia GPUs may require significant troubleshooting
    - ATI GPUs have not been formally tested
- TPM with proper BIOS support (required for **Anti Evil Maid**)
- A non-USB keyboard or multiple USB controllers

The installation process

After preparing the installation media (USB/DVD),

1. Boot the computer from it.
2. You'll receive the following screen, where you should choose one of the displayed options (**Test this media & install Qubes** will verify the target installation media for compatibility):

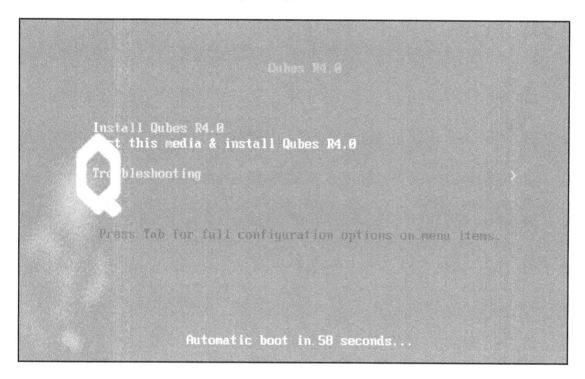

Install Qubes

3. You'll then see the installation process begin, starting with the installation of Xen on the computer. This will be in a **console/shell** view. When that process ends, you'll see the following screen:

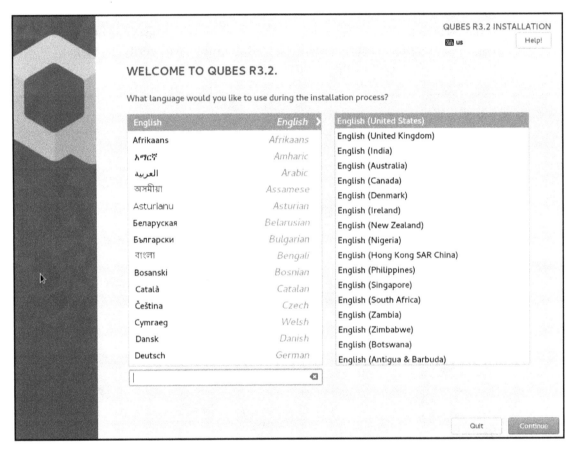

Welcome to Qubes

4. Choose the language you want and then press **Continue**:

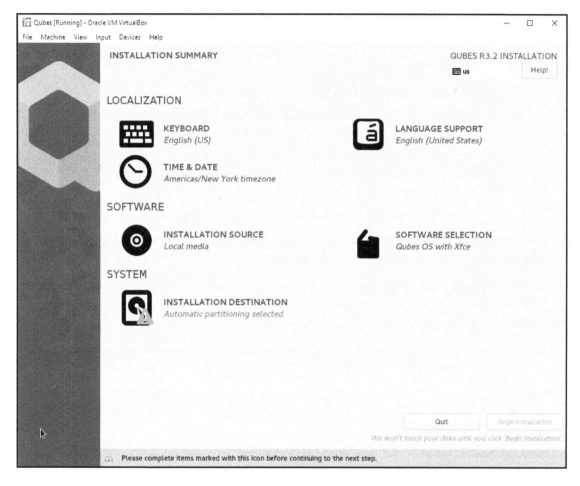

After a short wait, you'll reach the previously displayed screen, where you'll need to finalize the installation process, by completing the marked options, **Installation Destination**, and then, on the following screen, provide a username and password. The installation process will proceed and, when it ends, you'll be able to log in.

Using Qubes to access the Dark Web with Tor Browser is a little different than other operating systems. In its latest versions, Qubes use Whonix as a secure way to access the Tor network. Whonix replaced TorVM (a VM dedicated to Tor access) as the way to access Tor on Qubes. We'll discuss Whonix in depth in the next chapter, but, for now, let's understand how it helps with Qubes.

Whonix is installed with Whonix-Gateway and Whonix-Workstation TemplateVMs, where the Gateway is the part that accesses the network (or, more specifically, Tor). Whonix was developed and designed to be run inside a VM and paired with Tor. This makes it a perfect fit for Qubes. To install Whonix in Qubes, you need to access dom0 first.

To do so, perform the following steps:

1. Go to the **Start** menu and click **Terminal Emulator**.
2. Press *Alt + F3*, and type the following, and then press *Enter* twice:

    ```
    xfce terminal
    ```

3. Right-click on the desktop and select **Open Terminal Here**, and then run the following:

    ```
    sudo qubesctl state.sls qvm.anon-whonix
    ```

This can take some time (up to 30 minutes or more), and there's no progress indicator, so be patient. Stopping the process will result in errors.

According to the Qubes website, if an error message appears stating that `qubesctl` doesn't exist or the command isn't recognized, then it's necessary to enable the testing repository and install `salt`. To do so, run the following:

```
sudo qubes-dom0-update --best --allowerasing --enablerepo=qubes-dom0-
current-testing qubes-mgmt-salt-dom0-virtual-machines
```

If you install Qubes R4 and above, you can choose to set up a DVM Template as a base for **disposable VMs** (a VM that will be disposed of, after use, for more security). To do so, run the following in dom0:

```
sudo qubesctl state.sls qvm.whonix-ws-14-dvm
```

Now, update both the Whonix-Gateway and the Whonix-Workstation Template VMs by running the following:

```
sudo apt-get update
```

Accessing the Dark Web with Qubes

To launch Tor Browser, run the following:

1. Qubes App Launcher (blue/grey "**Q**") | Domain: anon-whonix | Privacy Browser
2. Now you can surf the Dark Web with Tor Browser, anonymously and privately, using Qubes OS (with a little help from Whonix), by entering the URLs of `.onion` sites into the browser address bar, as you would in a *standard* browser.

 Always remember, do NOT provide your real details on the Dark Web: not your name, address, emails, and definitely not your credit card details.

Even though we're discussing how to access the Dark Web in a more secure and private manner, remember the cardinal rule: do not trust software! They all have inherent vulnerabilities and can be exploited by attackers. Using security, privacy, and anonymity-focused operating systems helps minimize the risk, but it's never enough.

Be careful.

Summary

In this chapter, we talked about Qubes OS, how to install it, and its basic use. We discussed what makes Qubes unique and how it helps protect the user's privacy and security. We saw how two different systems work together (Qubes and Whonix), to provide an encompassing secure way to access the Dark Web.

In the next chapter, we'll discuss Whonix, another security-focused OS, but with a different approach.

Questions

1. What makes Qubes unique?
2. How can you differentiate between various qubes?
3. What hypervisor platform allows Qubes to create its qubes?

   A. Xen

   B. VMWare

   C. Hyper-V

Further reading

Please refer to the following reference:

- Qubes OS: https://www.qubes-os.org/

What Goes on in the Dark Web - Case Studies

9

In the last few chapters, we've discussed *how* to access the Dark Web securely and anonymously by installing and using various security- and privacy-focused operating systems, together with private browsers and VPNs.

In this chapter, let's discuss *what* goes on in the Dark Web, so you can decide *why* you want to go there. We'll discuss how the Dark Web is used, and talk about the stories (true or not) of what goes on in the Dark Web. Some of these examples will be graphic and detailed (not for the faint of heart), but most importantly, they are not of my invention.

I will retell tales that I've heard, read about, or have direct experience with.

Not all of them will be scary, morbid, or gross. Some will be of a positive nature, outlining how people put the Dark Web to use for whistle-blowing, sharing information, marketing, buying and selling, providing medial help, and much more.

We will cover the following topics in this chapter:

- The good and evil sides of the Dark Web
- Onion websites
- Illegal sales on the Dark Web using Bitcoin

The good and evil side of the Dark Web

Most of what we hear in the media is about criminal activities, such as drugs, weapons, and human trafficking, but in reality, there are many other benevolent and beneficial ways to use the Dark Web.

It's important to understand that the Dark Web provides an environment where people can express themselves freely and without censure (for better or worse), gain access to knowledge or content which otherwise would be very expensive to obtain (or even criminal), and find similarly-minded people, subcultures or hobbies (or any other uniting factor).

As with any tool or technology (and yes, I know I'm paraphrasing), the Dark Web isn't inherently evil.

It's populated by people, and it is these people who use the Dark Web for good or evil. Some say that the original intent of the Dark Web was to be an online Utopia, populated by people of every nation, religion and gender, sharing information freely, and working together for the benefit of all.

Sounds like a science fiction story, I know, but it is a worthy dream, nonetheless.

Somewhere along the way, the criminal element inserted itself (or people simply saw how easy it was to perform criminal activities anonymously on the Dark Web), and since shortly after its creation, the Dark Web has had a negative reputation.

The fact that it's called the Dark Web doesn't necessarily mean that it's evil, but the media and marketers have assigned evil or nefarious qualities to the Dark Web, to enhance sales or consumption of media. What makes the Dark Web so mysterious is the fact that it's not as accessible as **Surface Web** sites. As I explained previously, to access the Dark Web, you need a special browser (Tor, for example), you need to take more precautions, and most importantly, you can't find sites or results from the Dark Web using conventional search engines.

These all enhance the anonymity and privacy that users can take advantage of when browsing the Dark Web.

So let's start. And remember, many of the stories and facts you'll read also exist outside the Dark Web, it's just harder know who you are there, but human nature will always be human nature.

Onion websites

Many companies have started creating websites in the Dark Web, mainly to allow access in countries where there might be prohibitions on using them openly. One example is Facebook, which in October 2014 announced that they had added a Dark Web version in order to prevent access issues that happened when Tor users accessed their accounts through Facebook's regular site. The Dark Web version also allows users from countries that limit access to Facebook to be able to enjoy the social network. The following screenshot displays the Facebook onion site:

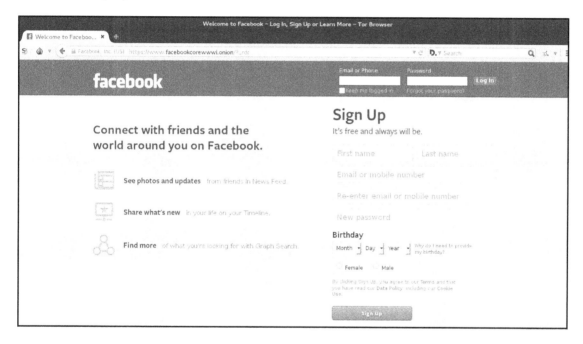

Several advertising companies also create sites in the Dark Web, to provide their services to users who want to view ads, but still want to maintain their privacy and security. As you may know, many ads collect information about us, and some are even considered malware. This is one of the reasons that adblockers were developed. For example, Adland, a site boasting the largest collections of Super Bowl commercials in the world, curates and displays ads and commercials from the whole world. They launched a Dark Web site, to protect their readers/surfers.

Here is a statement from the founder of Adland:

> *"Adland's target cares about privacy. We have two different types of readers. There are people who work in advertising, and then there are a lot of technical people like gamers who already have adblock installed."*

Additionally, she stated, *The way ad networks (on the Surface Web) are today are basically indistinguishable from malware. There's a lot of third-party calls going on between the publication that you're reading and the [tracker] on the publication.* She views the Dark Web as a mega adblocker, preventing the tracking of data with cookies.

So you could say that hosting an ad site on the Dark Web helps ensure that the ads are legitimate and do not contain malware or cookie-collecting options.

The following picture is of the Adland website:

ProPublica, an American independent, Pulitzer prize winning, nonprofit news site that produces investigative journalism dedicated to exposing incidents and stories that betray the public trust, also launched a Dark Web site, which makes it easier for whistle-blowers and other people who want to share news anonymously to disseminate their information.

The following screenshot is of ProPublica's website:

Everyday users, who began receiving web-search-based targeted ads, started looking for a way to keep their search habits private. Anonymous commerce is something that Facebook, Google, and others view as a significant threat, since one of their best marketing tactics is to monitor users' searches, and track them, followed by targeted ads.

As I indicated previously, dissidents and activists in oppressive regimes use the Dark Web to communicate so they don't get in trouble with their government – sadly there are still governments that limit outside communication through standard channels – or to report what they are experiencing to the outside world.

A report by the Human Rights Watch, a global non-profit, non-governmental human rights organization, called *Race to the Bottom: Corporate Complicity in Chinese Internet Censorship* actually discusses this and recommends that human rights workers throughout the world use the Dark Web to communicate securely and privately.

The following screenshot is of the Human Rights website:

In East Asia, Tor is used to ensure anonymity when people reveal information about sweatshops and other labor law problems.

Many situations that you hear about, or see in movies and TV shows, such as fighting the domination of a local town in the eastern US by a large corporation, is done via the Dark Web, by rallying local residents, and planning their actions anonymously and privately.

Human rights activists, working in dangerous areas, use the Dark Web to anonymously report abuse while avoiding prosecution.

Bloggers use Tor for anonymity, and band together to help each other and to promote freedom of speech. An example is Global Voices, an international and multilingual community of volunteering bloggers, journalists, translators, academics, and human rights activists. Their aim is to leverage the power of the internet to build understanding across borders.

They have a newsroom team to report on topics that rarely reach the regular media channels, and they translate the reported stories into numerous languages to break down language barriers.

The following screenshot is of the Global Voices website:

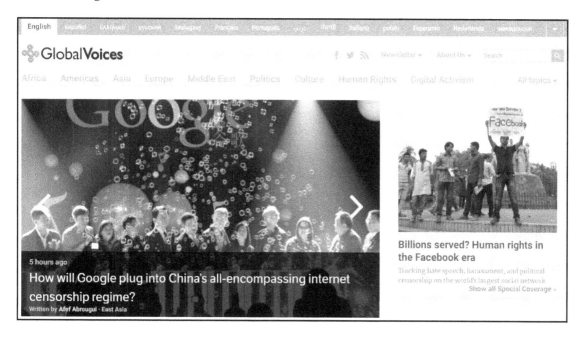

They also have a team advocating freedom of speech online. Called Advox, they're part of Global Voices, and according to their website, they *report on threats to online speech, share tactics for defending the work and words of netizens, and support efforts to improve Internet policy and practice worldwide.*

The following screenshot is of the Advox website:

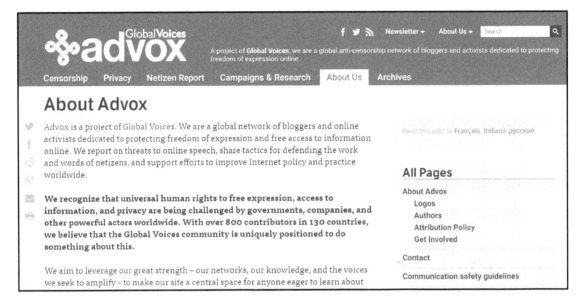

Another team, called Rising Voices, aims to provide training, resources, micro-grant funding, and mentoring to underrepresented communities that want to share their stories using media such as blogs, wikis, media sharing (video/audio/photos), podcasts, and vlogs.

The following screenshot is of the Rising Voices website:

Journalists use the Dark Web to communicate with their sources anonymously, and many news companies (such as The Washington Post, The New York Times, CBC, ProPublica, Dagbladet, and the Associated Press), have lockboxes there, such as SecureDrop, for people to send information and tips to in a secure and anonymous manner. An example of a Dark-Web-based news organization is Reporters without Borders, which is an organization that fights for freedom and protects journalists worldwide.

Lawyers, investigators, and reporters investigating governments use it to avoid being hacked or prosecuted.

The following screenshot is of the SecureDrop website:

Another common use for the Dark Web is to obtain medical advice and medical drugs. Some people are embarrassed to approach a doctor they know and ask questions, and not having to reveal your true identity can help ease that anxiety. Others ask about the possible dangers of combining different drugs, and even just asking about drugs they were prescribed, their effectiveness, side effects, and more. Others attempt to obtain drugs they need and wouldn't have the opportunity to obtain otherwise.

A well-known story revolves around DoctorX, also known as Dr. Fernando Caudevilla, from Madrid, Spain, who provides volunteer medical and drug advice on the Dark Web.

Working as a family physician by day, by night he's answered over 1,000 questions about drugs in forums on Silk Road 1, Silk Road 2, and The Hub.

DoctorX believes drugs should be a question of personal freedom and advocates legalization.

He works for Energy Control, a Spanish organization focused on harm reduction for recreational drug users.

The following screenshot is of the Energy Control website:

Now what about normal people? Many people use the Dark Web to find information or media that would be harder to find, or too expensive to buy on the Surface Web.

Tor and the Dark Web help protect our privacy while we're online. Sadly, many legitimate organizations can have unscrupulous employees, selling our private information. For example, ISPs sell customers' browsing information and history (which includes any search performed, website visited, and possibly usernames and passwords) to marketing companies, after supposedly anonymizing the data, something that is not always correct. Sadly, this information can also be obtained from the search engines we use, the social networks we're members of, and the websites we visit.

Many of you may have heard of GDPR, the European General Data Protection Regulation, a regulation focused on data protection and privacy for all individuals within the **European Union** (**EU**) and the **European Economic Area** (**EEA**).

GDPR was created to give individuals control over their personal data and to provide regulations to businesses regarding how to treat the personal data of their employees, customers, or business partners. GDPR applies to an enterprise established in the EEA or – regardless of its location and citizenship – that is processing the personal information of individuals or businesses inside the EEA.

GDPR requires these businesses to put in place *appropriate measures, both technical and organizational* to implement the data protection principles it provides, and to use the highest-possible privacy settings by default. This ensures the data is not publicly available without explicit, informed consent from the individuals, and that the data cannot be used to identify them without additional information, which is stored separately.

These measures already exist on the Dark Web, by default, especially if you use Tor or another darknet, which is why many people use them – to prevent the betrayal of their private data.

The vast majority of Dark Web users are privacy- and anonymity-focused people, so unless you provide information yourself, decline to use the standard precautionary measures we've discussed (which is comparable to explicit, informed consent), or if you're maliciously attempting to collect information about people, you'll actually be implementing GDPR, de facto – using appropriate measures to protect personal data.

The following screenshot is of the EU GDPR website:

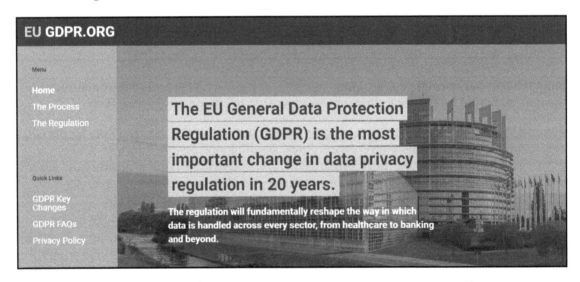

Additional uses of Tor (both on the Dark Web and the Surface Web) include protecting children, by obfuscating their IP address and preventing anyone from detecting the child's location. Naturally, Dark Web access should be regulated by parents, to prevent their children from accidentally (or intentionally) accessing the less-savory and illegal sites that exist there, but using Tor on the Surface Web is good enough.

Since one of the original goals of the Dark Web was information sharing, without censorship, there's a lot of it there. Many people perform research on any number of subjects, which might be sensitive and thus marked for monitoring by the NSA or any other governmental agency around the globe, or simply because they don't want to expose the information they're researching to their friends and family.

Many public figures have private blogs, forums, or websites on the Dark Web, allowing them to communicate their ideas and beliefs without compromising their public image. This is true for celebrities, political figures, and basically any person who is in the public eye.

Now, what about information sharing? There are many communities that share training and guides, regarding any number of subjects, from criminal activities such as hacking, counterfeiting documentation, and manufacturing drugs or other illegal substances, to deep-sea fishing and poetry discussions.

WikiLeaks is a site that is infamous for its political and corporate leaks, whose information is gleaned mainly via the Dark Web, with them posting that information on their Surface Web site.

The following screenshot is of the WikiLeaks website:

There are also many sites that are book clubs or that offer books, such as Bibliomaniac. It's said that you can find any book in the world on their website, but be careful and don't do anything illegal, such as downloading copyrighted content.

Just like on the Surface Web, music is accessible on the Dark Web, but much more so. Almost all of it is free.

Some Dark Web sites just display pictures or slideshows, such as Tor Kittenz, while others display reprehensible content, such as live tortures, murders, and kidnappings, and even worse things. I've heard of some that display images of injuries and accidents (similar to Ogrish or Gorish on the Surface Web, but worse, if that's possible). Sites displaying dead bodies, in general, are not so rare. And others allow you to get answers on truly anything. Hidden Answers, for example, is the Dark Web version of Reddit, where you can ask or share anything you want.

The following screenshot is of the Hidden Answers website:

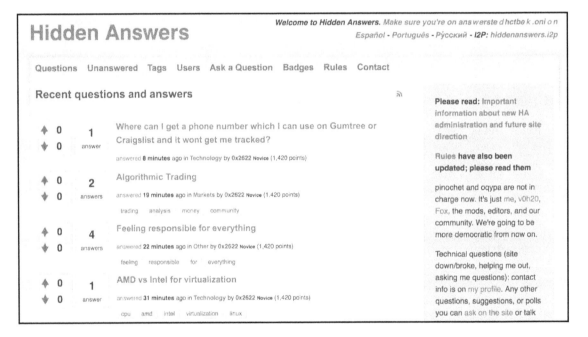

Illegal sales on the Dark Web using Bitcoin

The sheer diversity of sites on the Dark Web is only limited by people's imagination. I've heard the Dark Web called many things. One of them is *eBay on steroids* or *eBay for criminals*.

The truth is that you can buy just about anything on the Dark Web, such as drugs, weapons, counterfeit documentation, and various additional illegal substances and services. Alongside that, you can buy anything you might find in legal stores or websites. From carrots and vegetables to electronic equipment, some sites sell jokes and gags, such as underage fake IDs – you can even find animals for sale, some of which are illegal.

But never, ever buy anything on the Dark Web with your credit card. Purchases on the Dark Web are performed using cryptocurrency (or digital currency), such as Bitcoin (to name the most well-known one – there a quite a few out there).

To use Bitcoin, users need to create an account and a Bitcoin wallet. The buyer sends Bitcoin from their wallet to the wallet of the seller. The transaction is done securely, verified with a private code that allows the seller to verify that the Bitcoin is legitimate and that it has indeed been transferred to their wallet. This is verified by blockchain. A blockchain is a list of financial records (blocks) linked together, using cryptography. You can think of a blockchain as a public digital ledger, which has no centralized management, is distributed between many computers, and is encrypted.

Each block has irrefutable information (or so it is believed) of the block before it, and after it, and holds the information of the transaction. Attempting to change this information will lead to attempts to change the information in the rest of the blocks in the chain, making it impossible to do so without a consensus from the other members on the chain.

Personal information isn't revealed, which is one of the reasons that digital currency is so successful on the Dark Web. Bitcoin is also exchangeable with *normal* official currency in almost every country.

The following screenshot is of the Bitcoin Organization website:

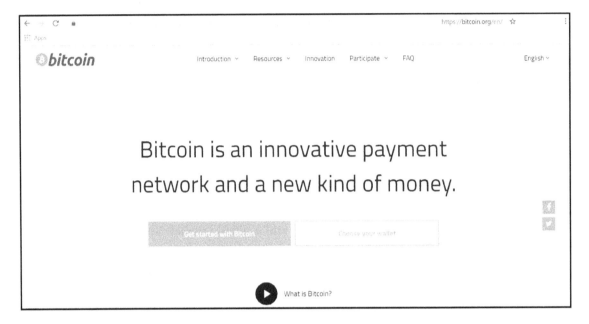

On July 15, 2015, an online dating service, called Ashley Madison, was hacked. The hackers sent the owners of the website a demand to shut down the site immediately. The demand was refused, so the hackers dumped all the data they had stolen, both corporate data, and personal, user data, on the Dark Web. Ashley Madison is now in the middle of a $576,000,000 class-action lawsuit.

All types of explicit content flourish on the Dark Web, from mundane to disgusting or horrifying.

A horrific site, called the Cruel Onion Wiki, has displayed the killing of animals. Although having been closed down multiple times, it keeps resurfacing.

A particularly well-known offer is of personal information (such as passwords, emails, IDs, and bank information). Some also offer to find specific information for you.

Most of us immediately think of hackers when we think of the Dark Web. There are many hackers on the Dark Web, not all of them are there to do bad. Some are merely learning and sharing information. But others are indeed there to offer their malevolent services. Many develop and sell cyber-weapons (such as general or specific exploits, malware kits, and botnets). Others provide cyber-attack services (such as DDoS attacks, hacking and defacement, and spam and malware distribution).

Nowadays, with easy access to information on how to perform exploits and to comparatively, easy to use malware (such as Trojans or ransomware), how to perform social-engineering attacks (such as spear-phishing). You can even rent a botnet for a specific amount of time. Unscrupulous people, under the cover of the Dark Web, can purchase or rent any of these and more, with almost no technical knowledge required (mainly if they purchase a service).

Drugs, is a topic that will have no end, if discussed, regarding the Dark Web. Any and every drug known to man is available for purchase there. Even very new, synthetic drugs are sold, but here the danger is even greater. Most of these drugs have never been properly tested and the Dark Web customers are, more often than not, the test subjects of these drugs.

Another industry that flourishes on the Dark Web is killers for hire. Many offer their services online, with the advertised, minimum fee of $20,000. It's said that the majority of these killers are actually law-enforcement officers, or scam artists.

Human and human-organ trafficking is also something you can find there, it's actually a very prolific topic, sadly, and many of the stories you may have heard, of people waking up in ice baths, with stitches in their sides, are based on this, with slavery not too far behind.

The Silk Road

Previously, I mentioned illegal sales on the Dark Web. You may have heard about a site called the Silk Road, which literally sold anything and everything, even things you would never want to think about. Launched in February 2011, it was shut down by the FBI in October 2013, who arrested its operator, Ross Ulbricht, also known as the *Dreaded Pirate Roberts*. Ulbricht was convicted and was sentenced to life in prison without the possibility of parole. Silk Road was relaunched on November 2013, operated by former administrators of the original Silk Road. It was shut down a year later, in a project called **Operation Onymous**, which was a 6-month-long international law-enforcement operation, including the police forces of 17 countries. It allegedly shut down over 400 sites participating in illegal activity, mainly the arbitration of sales of illegal products, including weapons, drugs, counterfeit currency, forged identity documents, stolen credit cards, and even murderers for hire. Among these sites were Agora, Evolution, and Andromeda, markets reputed to be even more nefarious than the Silk Road.

Terrorism

Sadly, the anonymous nature of the Dark Web allows terrorists to act undetected.

The Dark Web enables terrorists to recruit new members, disseminate propaganda, communicate with them on a regular basis, deliver orders, and organize the transfer of contraband – all with a low risk of being detected.

It's been found that white supremacy groups and even ISIS use the Dark Web for all of these activites, while ISIS even uses Dark Web sites to post videos of executions that they didn't publish publicly.

Summary

Like any technology, from coffeemakers to cellphones, the Dark Web can be used both for good and for evil. The fact that anonymity is held practically sacred there has many effects. The Tor project is based on the belief that anonymity is a requirement for a free and functional society.

Also, according to the Tor Project website, the majority of Dark Web activity is not centered on illegal activity. Only about 1.5% of traffic on the Dark Web is related to illegal activity (such as sales and services).

And due to the illegal activity, there are a lot of undercover law-enforcement agents all over the Dark Web. The anonymity that criminals enjoy on the Dark Web makes it equally easy for the police to find and stop them. Due to the nature of the Dark Web, it's nearly impossible to know who you're communicating with. The police can and go undercover, posing as a member of any number of professions, such as drug dealers or killers for hire.

Online stings occur, after people looking for a fix or someone to murder someone for them, get caught by the undercover agents.

The FBI, CIA, and NSA have all been confirmed to have a presence on the Dark Web.

Also, there are whitehat hackers that provide tech support, and assist in preventing crimes and locating perpetrators.

Questions

1. What is the name of the infamous Dark Web market that was led by the Dread Pirate Roberts?

    A. The Copper Road

    B. The Silver Road

    C. The Silk Road

    D. The Silk Street

2. What is the EU's Privacy Protection regulation called?

    A. General Data Protection Regulation

    B. Global Data Protection Rule

    C. General Direct Protection Regulation

    D. Global Data Protection Rule

3. What is Dr.X's real name?

    A. Dr. Felix Halfonella

    B. Dr. Fernando Caudevilla

    C. Dr. Figaro Cauvelli

    D. Dr. Fernando Caudwell

4. What prize did ProPublica win?

    A. Nobel

    B. Erasmus

    C. Pulitzer

    D. Oscar

Further reading

The following resources might be of interest if you'd like to dive deeper into the subjects covered in this chapter:

- https://sapas.sk/en/doctorx/
- https://motherboard.vice.com/en_us/article/ypwxwj/doctorx-is-the-darknets-most-reliable-drug-counselor
- https://www.hrw.org/reports/2006/china0806/
- https://eur-lex.europa.eu/legal-content/EN/TXT/HTML/?uri=CELEX:32016R0679from=EN
- https://ec.europa.eu/info/law/law-topic/data-protection_en
- https://bitcoin.org/

The Dangers of the Dark Web 10

The Dark Web has a bad reputation. Everyone has heard something about things that go on there. Sadly, the media has blown the stories out of proportion. As I've stated several times in this book, the main issues for the standard user are how you access it (dedicated browser) and the anonymity gained on it. So many of the stories you've heard of are exaggerated and aren't true.

But, there is a kernel of truth in the stories, and it's these that you need to be aware of.

This chapter will dive into these stories of the dangers on the Dark Web.

We will be covering the following topics in this chapter:

- Online scams
- Minimizing the risks on a Dark Web market
- Dangers of the Dark Web

Online scams

One of the dangers that exist both on the Surface Web and the Dark Web are scams.

Scams on the Dark Web are many and varied. Scams on Dark Web markets are common, as are ones performed by independent sellers

I'll talk about some of these in this chapter.

But one of the dangers are *index* sites, such as the Hidden Wiki. It's a site, founded in 20111, that lists links to Dark Web sites. It went down in 2013, but it was cloned and still works.

Although most of the links are valid (people pay money to list their Dark Web site there), there are sites which are posted there for the sole purpose of scamming people, and stealing their money.

Never, ever provide or write your debit or credit card numbers while on Dark Web sites. Never provide your true personal information. Since there's no real way of verifying someone's identity on the Dark Web, it's safer to hide your own.

That's part of anonymity and being anonymous

The following screenshot is of the Hidden Wiki:

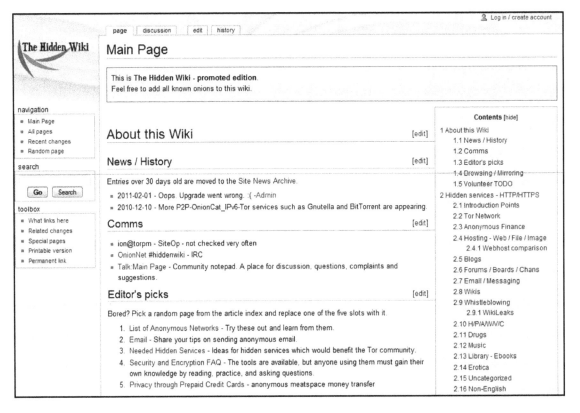

Screenshot of Hidden Wiki website

After being on the Dark Web for a while, you'll probably get a feel for the bad and illegal sites. That doesn't mean that you should let your guard down. Even on legitimate sites, the content you can view there can sometimes be unnerving.

Horrible videos, various types of services, and products from the disgusting to the perverse, can be found. Be careful if you have a weak stomach or are sensitive. Don't just click links. Try to read up about the site you want to access.

Also, many links can lead to malicious sites

And as a parent myself—don't let your children have free access to the Dark Web.

On the other hand, if you're looking to hire an assassin, you're probably out of luck. Most of those sites that advertise murder-for-hire services are fake.

Hitmen don't offer their services in such an overt manner. You can communicate with them on the Dark Web, but you can't just look them up.

These sites either run by law enforcement agencies, to capture people planning murder, or by scammers who demand between 15,000-25,000 US dollars, receive the money and vanish, or blackmail the person who paid them.

The market for fake IDs, social security numbers, credit cards, and other fake credentials is massive.

But not all of them are legit. Some of them are provided by scammers, who deliver bogus fake IDs, which crumble, even under the lightest scrutiny.

One of the problems are that the sites that offer these fake credentials, look professional, and feel legitimate. We've been conditioned to view sleek-looking sites as professional and proper. But in some situations, they can be malicious.

The following is a screenshot from a website that sells fake IDs:

Website selling Fake IDs

Here is another website that sells fake IDs online:

[LIMITED TIME SALE!] - MARYLAND Fake IDs | (Holos, UV, Barcode)
฿0.201288   ⭐ (320)

ships from: United States
ships to: United States   sold by Ethereal-IDs `94`

New Jersey Drivers License Holograms UV Scannable Fake ID
฿0.274082   ⭐ (188)

ships from: United States
ships to: Worldwide   sold by Good-IDs `78`

HQ Illinois ID. All Security Features. Great Service.
฿0.345494   ⭐ (169)

ships from: Undeclared
ships to: Worldwide   sold by ShopWithUs `94`

BEST Quality Fake California ID Anywhere – Scan/UV/Bend Test/Holos [TEMPORARY HALF PRICE SALE THIS WEEK ONLY]
฿0.480687   ⭐ (54)

ships from: United States
ships to: United States   sold by PowderBlue `96`

People have had their PayPal accounts stolen on sites like these, thinking that using PayPal would somehow be safer. You should find sites where trusted vendors sell. They should be multisig, for starters.

Another example of a scam, was during the Trump election. A Dark Web site was created, proclaiming that for enough money, they would assassinate President-elect Trump. Bitcoin was accepted for the fundraiser, but since the site was shut down, the exact amount of money collected is unknown. Naturally, nothing happened, but the admins took advantage of the wave of negativity toward President Trump during the elections.

Another scam was performed by Evolution Marketplace. Their admins scammed the users. They stole over 12 million dollars in Bitcoin and disappeared.

The following screenshot is from Evolution Marketplace:

The DeepDotWeb website lists several market sites which are supposedly legitimate (even proper sites can have problematic links), as can be seen in the following screenshot:

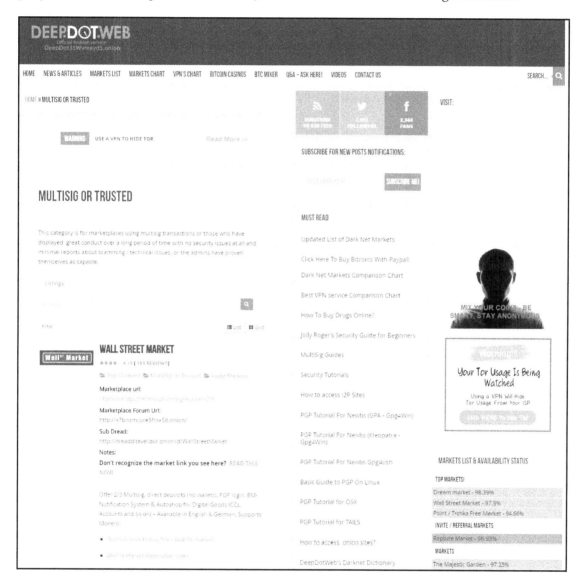

The Dark Web News website compiled a list of trusted vendor markets, according to their reputation.

Although I've accessed several of them, taking the precautions we've discussed in this book, with no ill effect, but as with all Dark Web sites, access them at your own risk.

You can see part of the list here:

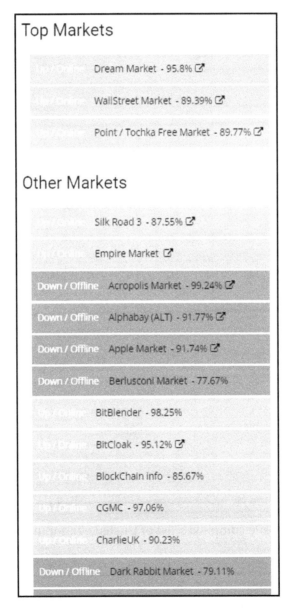

Also, they prepared a comparison between these sites, as shown in the following screenshot:

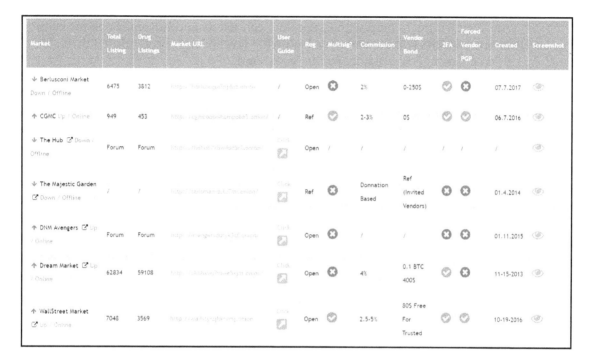

Market	Total Listing	Drug Listings	Market URL	User Guide	Reg	Multisig?	Commission	Vendor Bond	2FA	Forced Vendor PGP	Created	Screenshot
↓ Berlusconi Market Down / Offline	6475	3812	https...	/	Open	✗	2%	0-250$	✓	✗	07.7.2017	👁
↑ CGMC Up / Online	949	453	http...	/	Ref	✓	2-3%	0$	✓	✓	06.7.2016	👁
↓ The Hub Down / Offline	Forum	Forum	http...	Click 🗗	Open	/	/	/	/	/	/	👁
↓ The Majestic Garden Down / Offline	/	/	http...	Click 🗗	Ref	✗	Donnation Based	Ref (Invited Vendors)	✗	✗	01.4.2014	👁
↑ DNM Avengers Up / Online	Forum	Forum	http...	Click 🗗	Open	✗	/	/	✗	✗	01.11.2015	👁
↑ Dream Market Up / Online	62834	59108	http...	Click 🗗	Open	✗	4%	0.1 BTC 400$	✓	✗	11-15-2013	👁
↑ WallStreet Market Up / Online	7048	3569	http...	Click 🗗	Open	✓	2.5-5%	80$ Free For Trusted	✓	✓	10-19-2016	👁

I'm providing it as an example and to discuss what you should look for when looking for a legitimate Dark Web market. I'm not endorsing or confirming the list or the comparison. The reason is that I haven't tried all of the sites.

Avoiding the risks on a Dark Web market

So what should you look for to minimize the risk on a Dark Web market?

- **Multisig, escrow, finalize early**: These mean that the market is serious about protecting your money.
- **Anonymity and security**: How secure are you and your account on the market? Does the site use PGP, 2-factor authentication, phishing, and DDoS protection? You can do this by reading up on the site, and looking for this information there, before signing up.

- **Reviews**: Reviews on various other sites (both on the Surface Web and the Dark Web) will provide information about a market's reputation.
- **Help and support**: Does the market have a support team? Are they responsive? Are they willing to help with issues between sellers and buyers? Look for Help or Support links on the website. Read what level of support is offered there. Send them a message, to see how fast they respond.
- **Uptime status**: One of the most important metrics and validations that you can find is: how long has the site been up? Most index or search sites on the Dark Web will display the uptime of the sites listed on them.
  You can also try sites like: `https://dnstats.net/` or `https://www.deepdotweb.com`

Dangers of the Dark Web

One of the dangers of the Dark Web is having our information uploaded and displayed there. This has happened to Facebook, British Airways, the Marriott hotel chain, and many more. I will talk about one or two in this chapter.

For example, a top investment firm was discovered to save their client's information on unsecure servers. The information included **Personally Identifiable Information** (PII), such as their social security information and bank account numbers. This information was published on the Dark Web, putting the clients (and the investment firm) at risk

A Middle Eastern website was found to have inadvertently leaked administrative level credentials and credentials for remote terminals in several countries, to the Dark Web (it is not known how or who did it). This was caught in time, but the danger is there.

A major US healthcare organization, who was monitored by a Dark Web threat intelligence company, was found to have sensitive human resources and internal network information available on the Dark Web due to an issue with the required credentials for the system that holds the information. This was remediated and no recurrence was detected.

Access

Most people World Health Organization want to access the Deep internet use Tor, a service originally developed by the us armed service science lab. consider Tor as an online browser like Google Chrome or Firefox. the most distinction is that, rather than taking the foremost direct route between your laptop and also the deep elements of the net, the Tor browser uses a random path of encrypted servers, conjointly called **nodes**. This permits users to attach to the Deep internet without concern of their actions being half-tracked or their browser history being exposed. Sites on the Deep conjointly use Tor (or similar package like I2P) to stay anonymous, which means you will not be able to discover who's running them or wherever they are being hosted.

Many users currently leverage Tor to browse each the general public net and also the Deep. Some merely don't need government agencies or maybe net **Service suppliers** (**ISPs**) to understand what they are observing on-line, whereas others have very little choice—users in countries with strict access and use laws are usually prevented from accessing even public sites unless they use Tor shoppers and **virtual personal networks** (VPNs). the identical is true for presidency critics and different outspoken advocates World Health Organization worry backlash if their real identities were discovered. Of course, namelessness comes with a dark facet since criminals and malicious hackers conjointly choose to operate within the shadows.

Use and Misuse

For some users, the Deep internet offers the chance to bypass native restrictions and access TV or moving-picture show services which will not be on the market in their native areas. Others go far to transfer pirated music or grab movies that are not nevertheless in theaters. At the dark finish of the net, meanwhile, things will get chilling, salacious and simply plain...strange. As noted by The Guardian, for instance, mastercard information is obtainable on the Dark internet for simply some bucks per record, whereas ZDNet notes that something from pretend citizenship documents to passports and even the services of skilled hit men is obtainable if you recognize wherever to seem. Interested parties also can grab personal details and leverage them to blackmail standard net users. contemplate the recent Ashley Madison hack—vast amounts of account information, together with real names, addresses and phone numbers—ended au fait the Dark internet available. This proves that, whether or not you do not surf the murky waters of the Dark internet, you'll be in danger of blackmail (or worse) if sites you frequently use are hacked.

Illegal medicine are a well-liked draw on the Dark internet. As noted by Motherboard, drug marketplace the Silk Road—which has been finish off, replaced, finish off once more and so rebranded—offers any style of substance in any quantity to interested parties. Business corporate executive, meanwhile, details a number of the strange belongings you will hunt down within the Deep, together with a DIY ablation kit and a virtual scavenger hunts that culminated within the "hunter" responsive a NYC payphone at three a.m.

Real Risks

Thanks to the utilization of encoding and anonymization tools by each users and websites, there is just about no enforcement presence down within the Dark. this implies anything—even material well outside the bounds of fine style and customary decency—can be found on-line. This includes offensive, felonious "adult" content that will seemingly scar the viewer forever. A recent Wired article, for instance, reports that eighty % of Dark internet hits are connected to paedophilia and erotica. Here, the notion of the Dark as a haven for privacy wears skinny and shores up the notion that if you are doing like better to go far, continually limit access to your Tor-enabled device thus youngsters or different relations are not in danger of unsteady across one thing nobody ought to ever see. Visit the Deep internet if you are interested, however do yourself a favor: do not let children anyplace close to it and tread carefully—it's a protracted manner down.

Some general dangers

Many Dark Web markets allow the illegal sales and purchasing of drugs, weapons, and according to several sources, even human trafficking. Since the markets are anonymous, this increases the danger—who are you really buying from? Are they reliable? Will they steal our money?

Credit card numbers, bank account information, and other personal information can be purchased on the Dark Web for us in theft and fraud activities. This can lead to counterfeiting of your documentation. Just another reason to keep your personal information off the Dark Web.

Black hat hackers brag about their exploits, communicate and collaborate with other hackers, and share security exploits on the Dark Web, where they can stay anonymous.

But another side of hackers' presence on the Dark Web is that they practice their craft there, trying to lure innocent users into doing something that will provide a weakness or an attack vector, which will allow them to hack the users.

Always be careful of links you are about to click. Never download or click executables or anything that looks fishy.

Malware is something that is prolific on the Dark Web. In 2017, there were several malware detected there; for example:

- 2017 – Karmen Ransomware RaaS
- 2017 – MACSPY – Remote Access Trojan as a service on Dark web
- 2017 – MacRansom is the first Mac ransomware offered as a RaaS Service.
- 2017 –Ransomware-as-a-Service dubbed Shifr RaaS that allows creating ransomware compiling three form fields.

Botnets are another danger on the Dark Web, especially Tor-based botnets. They can show the following:

- Availability of authenticated hidden services
- Availability of private Tor networks
- Possibility of exit node flooding

Security researchers try to detect botnets and their Command and Control servers (C&Cs), by performing traffic analysis. This is done with **Intrusion Detection Systems (IDS)** and network analyzers. To remove a botnet, the following actions can be taken:

- Cleaning the C&C servers and infected hosts
- Revoking domain names
- Obscurating the IP addresses assigned to the C&C server

Since the botnet traffic is routed through the Tor network, it's encrypted, which makes it hard to analyze.

Tor-based botnets can masquerade as legitimate Tor traffic and encryption prevents most intrusion detection systems from detecting botnets. In addition, the C&C servers are hard to find. The operator can easily move around the C&C servers just by re-using the generated private key for the hidden service that the botnet uses.

Gamblers love the Dark Web, as it allows them to feed their addiction or allow them to play their games, without regard of local gambling laws, especially if the games are illegal.

As I've discussed in other chapters, terrorists use the Dark Web for communication, recruiting, and organizing (themselves and their attacks). This is very difficult to detect, and monitor, which is the main reason that they use the Dark Web.

Another danger is being blamed of wrongdoing or illegal acts. As I've already mentioned, law enforcement agencies create Dark Web sites to draw in people and apprehend them, if they commit a crime.

The problem is that sometimes innocent people access illegal sites, or even use content that they didn't know was illegal, and then they are arrested, even though they didn't do anything wrong, at least not intentionally.

Also, ISPs and governments are devising ways to monitor the Dark Web for illegal activity. Since it's sometimes hard to differentiate between criminals and legitimate users, this is alarming.

NASA, for example, have been working on a search engine to track illegal activities, as you can see in the following screenshot:

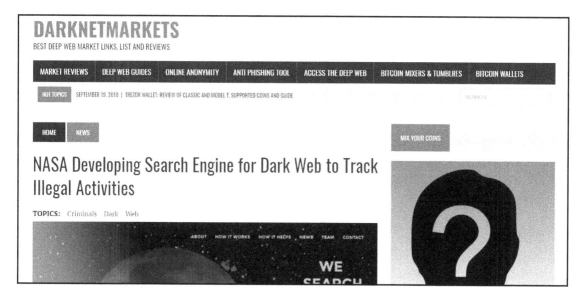

There can always be a downside to every technology.

Sadly, anarchists, weapon dealers, perverts, drug dealers, and other horrible people are on the Dark Web. The danger here is more of a mental one. Being exposed to awful images or videos, or any other type of content, can harm people.

Summary

In this chapter, we discussed some of the dangers that exist on the Dark Web. We also discussed best practices and how to protect ourselves.

The main takeaway from this chapter, in my eyes, is that even though danger exists on the Dark Web, it exists elsewhere as well. And if you take the necessary precautions, and are careful, there's no reason why you can't enjoy the wealth of information and topics, which can be found on the Dark Web.

Use it responsibly, privately, and for good reasons, and you will be fulfilling the dream that the Dark Web is, for all people who want to communicate privately, and without fear of having their private information leaked.

Questions

1. Which of the following constitute Dark Web dangers?

    A. Malware

    B. Bombs

    C. Tor botnets

    D. Assassinations

2. Which government agency developed a search engine for illegal activity?

    A. NSA

    B. FBI

    C. CIA

    D. NASA

3. What metrics should you verify to make sure a Dark Web market is legitimate?

Further reading

The following resources might be interesting if you'd like to go deeper into the subjects covered in this chapter:

- https://www.tandfonline.com/doi/full/10.1080/23738871.2017.1298643?scroll=topneedAccess=true
- https://darkwebnews.com/malware/malware-spreading-by-stenography/
- https://resources.infosecinstitute.com/malware-dark-web/#

Using the Dark Web for Your Business

11

In the previous chapter, I enumerated case studies and use cases of the Dark Web. As you've seen, there are many ways that people use the Dark Web.

One might say that you can use the Dark Web in the same way as you use the Surface Web, while the main difference is which browser you use to access the sites: searching for information, consuming content (music, audio, video, written content, and more), participating in social networks, posting content, and communicating.

Also, if you access to the Dark Web in the proper manner, you will be anonymous and able to protect your privacy, something that is much harder on the Surface Web, due to its design and architecture (and use—think about targeted ads, for example).

In this chapter, I'll be focusing on business uses of the Dark Web, and maybe provide readers with insights on how to utilize the Dark Web for their own organizations. My goal in this chapter is to provide ideas and use cases that can benefit businesses, based on common and personal experience.

The anonymity and privacy that is gained by using Tor or any other *Dark Web browser* allows businesses to perform actions that would otherwise expose them and the information they were looking for, thus even harming them financially or their good name.

In this chapter, we will be talking about the following types of users who access the Dark Web for different purposes:

- IT professionals
- Law enforcement agencies
- Business companies
- Military organizations
- Cybersecurity professionals

IT professionals

I'll start with IT professionals. They are usually the closest to the Dark Web, and feel the most comfortable accessing it, either because of their vocation, or simply out of curiosity.

They know how to use the tools that allow safe access to the Dark Web, such as VPNs and Tor.

Many IT professionals need to access materials on the internet for their work, which may violate strict company procedures, such as not being allowed to access site X using organizational browsers. This is a tricky situation, since they can't perform their work without violating the procedure/policy.

This is a type of catch-22.

To resolve this, IT professionals can use the Tor Browser (or other *Dark Web browsers*), which won't alert the organizational security systems of this action, due to the way Tor works.

Additionally, if the IT professionals do this on a regular basis, they usually have a dedicated machine ready for Dark Web access, which also minimizes their risk of exposing the organization (monitoring search terms helps attackers' information-gathering, so if they can't monitor the searches, this minimizes the attack surface), which would naturally clash with the original intent—preventing organizational information from leaking while attempting to collect important information. These dedicated machines would have a secure OS installed on it, such as the ones we discussed in previous chapters, have a VPN installed, and all traffic would be configured to go through Tor.

They can also use Tor to verify their IP-based firewall rules, such as to test rules that allow or block specific IP addresses or ranges. The IT professionals can use Tor to verify that the rules are effective, since it doesn't use an IP from the organizational ranges. This can be done in a variety of scenarios—checking whether external IPs have access to internal resources, checking whether organizational **Network Access Control systems** (**NACs**) are working effectively by preventing access to organizational resources from IP ranges that aren't in the organizational pool, or even by preventing access from MAC addresses that aren't recognized by the organization.

Sometimes **Internet Service Providers** (**ISPs**) have network issues, such as problems with DNS resolution or routing issues, so if this happens, IT people can use Tor to access resources on the internet, providing business continuity.

In the same manner, an IT professional can connect to services without having to use an external machine or account. This depends on the nature of the network issue, of course. Not all of these issues can be overcome by using Tor, but many can, so be aware and always assess the situation.

Many business people access the Dark Web, using Tor, for many reasons, for example to view competitors' websites without being affected by any rules that are in place on the website, such as displaying misinformation to machines accessing it from specific IP ranges or sources. As you know already, Tor obfuscates the IP of the source machine, preventing detection, and allowing the user to access resources, both on the Dark Web and the Surface Web, with a very low chance of detection (if precautions are taken, of course).

The Dark Web is a treasure trove of hidden or raw data. So, companies research scientific and business topics there, providing valuable insights on their business, their customers, and their competition. The data there is usually unfiltered, and unbiased, which helps them to make more informed decisions.

Business companies

Many organizations create security-breach information repositories (clearinghouses) to collect information about breaches and breach attempts. Then they correlate the information and try to detect patterns or definitive information, which will allow them to better protect themselves, mitigate risk, and alert internal security teams, or even similar companies, to these attacks.

Also, these repositories are prime targets for attackers, so managing them on the Dark Web provides protection from detection and exfiltration of the information and their source IPs.

Organizations that are employee-focused use the Dark Web as a place in which employees can report to management on irresponsible or illegal activity performed inside the organization, without fear of repercussion.

Many companies also have analysts who monitor various websites for information that can help them. Naturally, they don't want their competitors to detect what they're watching (to prevent industrial espionage) and to compile patterns or information about them, so they use Tor for this.

We've been focusing on the Dark Web, but it's important to remember that there's a lot of information also on the Deep Web, located in organizational databases and systems, which are simply not indexed by search engines, and which can be accessed by either using a dedicated search system, or by signing up and logging into the organizational systems.

Several such examples are as follows:

- **DeepDyve**: A site that aggregates millions of scholarly articles, only accessible if you sign up:

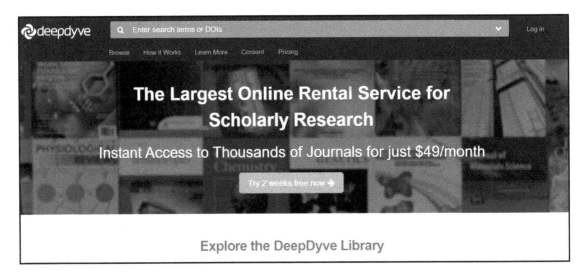

- **Academic Index**: A site that provides access to Deep Web academic sites:

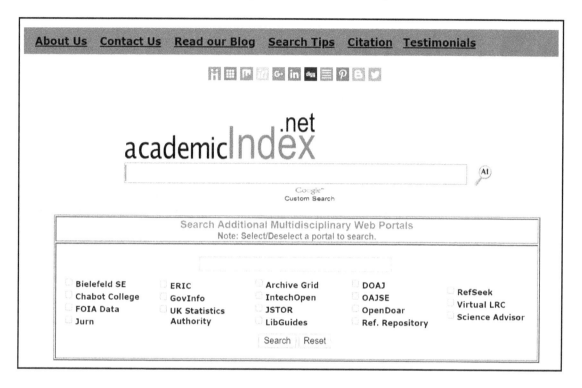

- **Sciencegov**: A site with scientific articles collected from US government agencies:

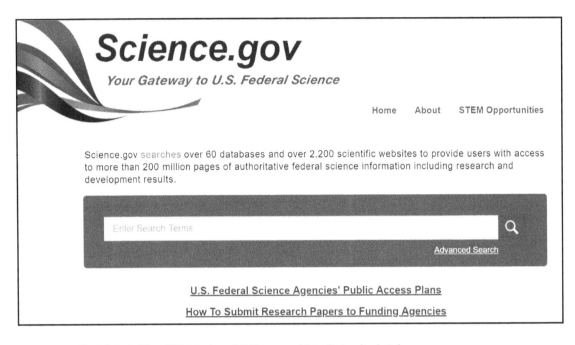

- **PubMed**: The US National Library of Medicine's database:

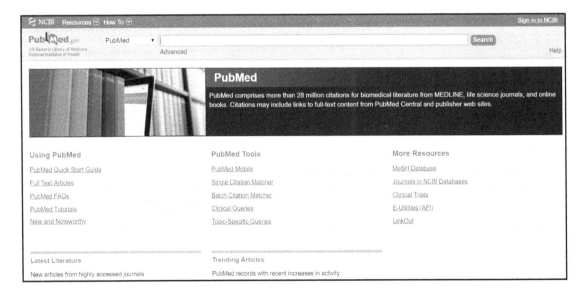

- **Law Library of Congress**: Claims to be the largest collection of legal materials in the world, with over 2,000,000 volumes available:

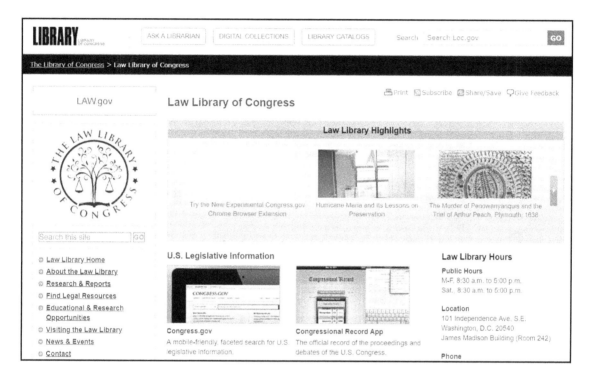

- **JSTOR**: One of the oldest online libraries. Members receive access to more than 12,000,000 academic journal articles, books, and primary sources in 75 disciplines:

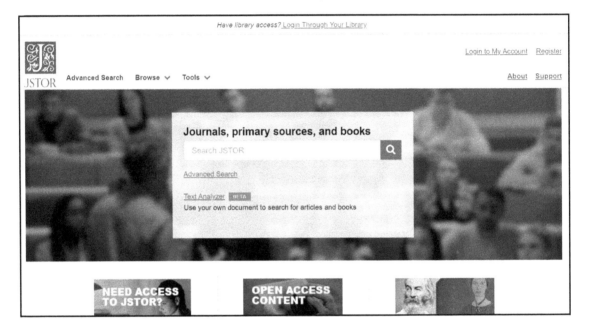

But there are many many more, of course.

Law enforcement agencies

As I wrote before, law enforcement agencies have a strong presence on the Dark Web. The officers working for these agencies can engage in undercover sting operations to capture criminals and other people engaged in illegal activity. Using Tor provides anonymity and hides the source IPs of the officers' computers, which otherwise would have blown their cover.

In the same manner, law enforcement agencies perform discreet online surveillance of services and websites without revealing themselves, by using Tor.

In order to better explain how law enforcement can operate on the Dark Web, I'd like to tell you about Operation Bayonet, a Dutch-led sting operation, to take down Hansa, a Dark Web market site, numbering 3,600 dealers offering more than 24,000 drug product listings, as well as fraud tools and counterfeit documents. They were able to monitor Hansa's buyers and sellers, using various tools and methods, and discreetly altered Hansa's code to grab additional information, which helped identify those users, and even tricked many of Hansa's anonymous sellers into opening a file on their computers that revealed their location to the investigators. During the investigation, both Surface and Dark Web capabilities were exploited by the investigators, using the anonymity provided, to discover Hansa's development server, where new features were tested before deploying them to the live site, taking control of it, and through it, finding the live site servers.

They copied the server's drives, including records of every transaction performed, and every communication that took place through its anonymized messaging system. This led them to discover the founders' IRC chat logs, which surprisingly, included the administrators names and even their home addresses.

Even though you might think that the operation ends here, there's more. The Dutch investigators wanted to try to capture vendors selling illegal goods through Hansa, so rather than arresting the site administrators immediately, they waited. This caused a setback in the operation, as the Hansa servers they had found vanished, but the site kept on working. They understood that they'd been discovered by the site admins. Rather than admitting defeat, the investigators invested months in going over all the evidence they had collected so far, and in April 2017, got a lucky break—a bitcoin payment had been made from an address that had included in the IRC chat logs they had discovered. By using blockchain-analysis software, the bitcoin payment provider was found to have an office in the Netherlands.

The police contacted the bitcoin payment company and obtained information about the payment recipient—a company in Lithuania.

Again, as fate would have it, the investigators paused before closing down the site, following a meeting with the FBI, who told them that they would be shutting down AlphaBay, one of the most popular drug markets on the Dark Web at the time.

This would cause the vendors and buyers to look for a new marketplace, and it would probably be Hansa. The Dutch police understood that this would put them in a position to apprehend many more drug dealers and people selling illegal goods than if they'd just shut down Hansa. They'd also be able instill a feeling of distrust in the safety of Dark Web markets, and that the law would be able to get them anywhere, even on the Dark Web.

In a joint action, German police arrested the two people suspected of being Hansa's admins, and were able to seize their hard drives. Then the Dutch police migrated the Hansa server's data to their own servers, effectively taking control of the site.

They then proceeded to rewrite the site code, logged the user's passwords, and unencrypted the messages on the site, discovering many buyers' home addresses.

They also removed a feature that anonymized photos, causing user metadata to remain embedded in the files, providing geolocation information that led to locating more than 50 drug dealers.

Files that acted as homing beacons were sent to sellers, designed to look like a backup key for bitcoin received on the website. Opening the file connected the sellers' devices to a specific URL, uncovering the sellers' IP addresses.

After Alphabay was closed in July 2017, over 30,000 drug buyers registered on Hansa, falling under police surveillance. The amount of newly-registered users became so great that the police stopped registration for nearly two weeks.

After 27 days of collecting information about the people buying and selling on Hansa, the Dutch police shut down the site, leaving a notice to anyone who might try to access it:

> *"We trace people who are active at Dark Markets and offer illicit goods or services,"* the site read. *"Are you one of them? Then you have our attention."*

Dozens of arrests were performed, over $12,000,000 in bitcoin was seized, in addition to the effect that it had on the Dark Web criminal element.

Also, in a massive sting operation in the US, law enforcement agents from a multiple state departments—including the Department of Justice, Homeland Security Investigations, the US Secret Service, the Postal Inspection Service, and the **Drug Enforcement Administration** (**DEA**)—apprehended and arrested over 35 dark web traders across the country, by posing as traders and vendors themselves.

Additionally, to ensure anonymous tips, posting them on the Dark Web, or even just using Tor, will keep the reporters anonymous.

Military organizations

Military organizations us the Dark Web for covert communications, protecting military actions, operations, and adhering to military information security procedures (such as non-disclosure).

It also allows military, governmental, and civilian intelligence, and counter-intelligence units to collect information without revealing themselves to the subjects of their research.

As you now know, the internet was originally designed and launched by DARPA, to ensure continued communication in case of attacks on the US, and to hide the physical location of the communicating objects, Tor was developed, based on this, and further ensures the above.

In an attempt to combat the use of the Dark Web for sex trafficking, DARPA built a search engine called Memex to try to find information and leads from the Dark Web.

It cost DARPA $67,000,000, and is in use by over 33 law enforcement agencies since 2014. It looks for online behavioral signals in ads and helps detect whether a person is being trafficked.

Even though it's extremely hard to collect information about a person on the Dark Web, signals exist in data, in online photos, and even in the text of ads.

Intelligence capabilities compare the information it collects to behaviors associated with trafficking, trying to understand the human trafficking footprint in online spaces.

> *"Our goal is to understand the footprint of human trafficking in online spaces, whether that be the dark web or the open web." – Wade Shen, a program manager in DARPA's Information*

Cybersecurity professionals

Cybersecurity professionals also use the Dark Web. They monitor sites, forums, and blogs, where hackers exchange information regarding new exploits and hacks, companies or individuals they've targeted, and more. This provides them with threat intelligence and insights into emerging threats, thus enabling them to better protect their organizations.

There are also many systems that collect threat intelligence, some collecting information from the Dark Web, such as Silobreaker, Webhose, RepKnight, Terbium labs, Massive, Recorded Future, Sixgill, Hold Security, and AlienVault, which provide information about new malware and exploits and also allow the user to detect whether there's jabber about a person or company, by searching for a credit card number or a social security number, among other capabilities. This allows them to detect new vulnerabilities and exploits, and also receive insights as to whether companies are being targeted or were hacked and had their information leaked.

If you remember, I mentioned that Facebook and other sites have a Dark Web presence. The business advantage is providing access to their services and business to citizens in countries where these types of sites are blocked, thus enlarging their customer base (and ultimately making more money).

Summary

In this book, we discussed how to access the Dark Web, the who, and the why.

You've seen that it's used for the best of reasons, and the worst...

As with all technology, it's neither good nor evil; it's how the technology is used that makes the difference.

The Dark Web is very similar to the Surface Web. The main difference is the anonymity and privacy, which are more pronounced on the Dark Web.

In this chapter, I tried to show you that the Dark Web can be very beneficial, and that law enforcement is working diligently to protect us, both off and on the Dark Web.

I hope that you see, as I do, the advantages of the Dark Web, rather than its dangers or disadvantages.

Use it, but on your own terms. Use it safely, use it wisely, and ultimately, it should benefit you.

Maybe renaming it to something less ominous might change the perception most people have of it, but as Shakespeare wrote, What's in a name?

Questions

1. What was the Dutch police's sting operation called?

   A. Operation Saber

   B. Operation Bayonet

   C. Operation Switchblade

   D. Operation Turnover

2. What do some tools look for on the Dark Web?

   A. Artificial Intelligence

   B. Business Intelligence

   C. Threat Intelligence

   D. Basic Intelligence

3. What advantages does the Dark Web offer to IT professionals?

   A. Accessing information that is located on sites which are usually blocked

   B. Testing security systems and firewall rules

   C. Overcoming network issues such as routing or DNS resolving

Further reading

The following resources might be of interest if you'd like to dive deeper into the subjects covered in this chapter:

- `https://en.wikipedia.org/wiki/Operation_Bayonet_(darknet)`
- `https://darknetdiaries.com/episode/24/`
- `https://go.recordedfuture.com/dark-web`

Assessment

Chapter 1: Understanding the Deep and Dark Web

1. Surface Web, Deep Web, Dark Web
2. Search engines
3. True
4. Private databases, News headlines, Academic journals
5. Darknets, Overlay networks, Content accessible using specialized software
6. Journalism, Sale of an exploit tool you have developed
7. Bypassing country censorships, Buying counterfeit money

Chapter 2: Working with the Deep Web

1. The privacy and anonymity are defined as follows:
   - **Privacy** can be defined as a state in which a person (or a corporate entity) can hide information about themselves from others. This can be done for various reasons, which ultimately don't matter. The idea is that it's possible, or at least should be. This is becoming enforced by laws, such as GDPR, or any number of privacy acts and laws
   - **Anonymity**, can be described as hiding a persons true identity from others without hiding or censoring their activities.

2. The three main cryptocurrency transaction methods are as follows:
   - **Finalize Early**: Is a payment method, in which a vendor requires receipt of payment before dispatching the purchased goods. The risk is on the buyer's end, but it also expedites the transaction due to little or no risk on the vendor's side (this method is the least secure for the buyer)
   - **Escrow**: Is a payment method in which a Dark Web market will generate a bitcoin address to which the buyer transfers the payment. The market holds the buyer's money and pay's the vendor only after the buyer marks the order as complete. (Moderately Secure)

- **Multiple Signature Escrow**: Also called multisig, this payment method generates multiple keys for the bitcoin transaction and payment release process. The multisig can be either 2 out of 2 or 2 out of 3, where 2 of 3 provides the most security for three keys - the market's key, the vendor's key and the buyer's key. The keys are:
  - **2-of-2 Multisig**: Market public key, vendor public key
  - **2-of-3 Multisig**: Market public key, vendor public key + customer public key

3. The Dark Web search websites are as follows:

   - Ahmia
   - Torch
   - DuckDuckGo

4. Almost everything you might do on the Surface Web (including Browsing, Email, Blogging, Forums, Financial Transacting)

Chapter 3: The Future of the Dark Web

1. Three improvements in Tor are:
   - Host websites anonymously and privately.
   - Onion domain names will include more characters.
   - The network will randomly assign the relays that each onion service contacts.

2. Dark Web markets are:
   - Hansa
   - Agora
   - OpenBazaar
   - Silk Road

3. Main proposed future changes in the Dark Web are:
   - The UI of applications designed to access the Dark Web, such as Tor, are becoming more user friendly
   - Enhanced security, privacy and anonymity
   - Making the Dark Web more mainstream

Chapter 4: Installing a Linux Virtual Machine (VM)

1. An open source, free OS, with an emphasis on relatively easy customization and security (among other features).
2. A distro (or distribution) is a version or flavor of Linux. The differences in distros mainly revolve around desktop interfaces, included software and technology, intended use, and other aspects. There is no best distro, but rather the best distro for you. Remember to try out several until you find the one that best fits your requirements and temperament.
3. Linus Torvalds

Chapter 5: Accessing the Dark Web with Tor Browser

1. Four recommendations for safe use of Tor Browser are:
   - Don't torrent over Tor.
   - Don't enable or install browser plugins.
   - Use HTTPS versions of websites.
   - Don't open documents downloaded through Tor while online.
2. Tor Browser is based on Firefox browser.
3. The following is the command:

   ```
   ./start-tor-browser.desktop
   ```

Chapter 6: Installing Tails OS

1. The Linux software installation requirements for Tails OS are as follows:
   - Debian 9 and higher
   - Ubuntu 16.04 and higher
   - Linux Mint 18 and higher
2. The Terminal command that starts the Tails Installer application is:

   ```
   sudo apt install tails-installer
   ```

3. The Tails OS hardware installation requirements are as follows:
   - A 64-bit x86-64 compatible processor (except for PowerPC or ARM)
   - 2 GB of RAM
   - A way to boot either from a DVD or USB flash drive

Chapter 7: Installing Whonix

1. The other operating system is designed to work with Whonix are as follows:
   - Qubes OS
   - Windows
   - Ubuntu Linux
   - Tails
2. Whonix is unique as:
   - Its architecture consist of two virtual machines, one acting as the secure and anonymous gateway, while the other functions as the user's desktop OS.
   - All traffic is routed through Tor, by default.
   - Whonix comes with anonymity and privacy focused applications installed by default.

Chapter 8: Installing Qubes OS

1. Qubes is unique as, it is based on the concept of isolation, where each application, hardware and session exist in different virtual machines, hence isolating them from one another, but still providing the user with a smooth, unified interface.
2. Each qube has its own window, and the windows have different color borders, to display the different level of security, and qube, being used.
3. The hypervisor platform that allows Qubes to create its qubes is: Xen

Chapter 9: What Goes on in the Dark Web - Case Studies

1. The Silk Road
2. General Data Protection Regulation
3. Dr. Fernando Caudevilla
4. Pulitzer

Chapter 10: The Dangers of the Dark Web

1. Malware and Tor botnets
2. NASA
3. Following are the metrics you should use to verify to make sure a Dark Web market is legitimate:
   - Multisig, Escrow, Finalize early
   - Anonymity and security
   - Reviews
   - Help and support
   - Uptime Status

Chapter 11: Using the Dark Web for Your Business

1. Operation Bayonet
2. Threat Intelligence
3. All A, B, C

Another Book You May Enjoy

If you enjoyed this book, you may be interested in these another book by Packt:

Learn Social Engineering
Erdal Ozkaya

ISBN: 978-1-78883-792-7

- Learn to implement information security using social engineering
- Learn social engineering for IT security
- Understand the role of social media in social engineering
- Get acquainted with Practical Human hacking skills
- Learn to think like a social engineer
- Learn to beat a social engineer

Leave a review - let other readers know what you think

Please share your thoughts on this book with others by leaving a review on the site that you bought it from. If you purchased the book from Amazon, please leave us an honest review on this book's Amazon page. This is vital so that other potential readers can see and use your unbiased opinion to make purchasing decisions, we can understand what our customers think about our products, and our authors can see your feedback on the title that they have worked with Packt to create. It will only take a few minutes of your time, but is valuable to other potential customers, our authors, and Packt. Thank you!

Index

used, for accessing Dark Web 137

R

Rufus
  reference 132
RVI
  reference 117

S

Scryptmail 37
security domain 130
SoylentNews 41

T

Tails OS
  about 99
  downloading 102
  downloading, in Linux 102
  downloading, in Windows 102
  installation prerequisites 101
  installing 103
  installing, from command line 106, 108, 109, 112
  installing, in Fedora 104
  installing, in Red Hat 104
  installing, on Windows 103
Tails
  about 32
  reference 102
The Amnesic Incognito Live System (Tails) 99
Tor (The Onion Router)
  about 82
  and I2P comparison, reference 16
  installing, entirely via Terminal 92
  installing, on Linux 83, 84, 86, 87, 89, 91
  installing, via Terminal 91
  reference 83
Tor bridge relay
  reference 93
Tor Browser
  using, with Whonix 126, 127
Tor Links 36

Tor Project
  about 55
  recommendations 95
  reference 93
Transport Control Protocol/Internet Protocol (TCP/IP) 8
tumblers 29

U

Ubuntu Desktop Edition
  reference 66
Uniform Resource Locators (URLs) 11
USB flash drive
  Linux VM, executing from 77, 78
users, Dark Web
  business companies 177
  cybersecurity professionals 185
  IT professionals 176
  law enforcement agencies 182, 183
  military organizations 184

V

Virtual Private Network (VPN) 93
VirtualBox
  download link 118

W

Whonix
  about 115
  benefits 116
  download link 118
  installation 117, 118, 121, 123, 124
  prerequisites 117
  Tor Browser, using with 126, 127
Wikileaks 41
Windows
  Tails OS, downloading 102
  Tails OS, installing 103
World Wide Web 11

Z

zero-day attacks 129